180 DAYS

of

CREATIVE WRITING

PROMPTS

HIGH SCHOOL
EDITION

**FICTION, NONFICTION, &
POETRY STARTERS FOR EVERY
DAY OF THE SCHOOL YEAR**

KELLY COON, M.ED.
USA TODAY BESTSELLING YA AUTHOR &
SECONDARY ENGLISH EDUCATOR

CASLMON
CLARK

This book is intended to provide helpful information on the subjects addressed. It is for educational purposes only. The author has made every effort to ensure that the material printed in this book is complete and accurate.

Audience: Ages 12 & up | Grades 9 & up

Published by Caslmon Clark.

Library of Congress Control Number (LCCN): coming soon

ISBN (paperback): 979-8-9938718-0-6
ISBN (ebook): 979-8-9938718-1-3

ALSO BY THE AUTHOR:

GRAVEMAIDENS
WARMAIDENS
TAKE UP SPACE, Y'ALL
PRANK NIGHT

www.kellycoon.com
@kellycoon106

CONTENTS

60 FICTION PROMPTS

60 NONFICTION PROMPTS

60 POETRY PROMPTS

INTRODUCTION

Dear Reader,

When I was a teenager, *starving* for creative writing resources, I was pretty much never fed. This was back in the dinosaur 90s before computers were even used in the classroom, so I relied on rewriting stories with which I was already familiar (giving them fierce female characters who rode dragons) or just scribbling ideas about my dragon-slaying epic heroism into spiral notebooks while the teacher was helping my classmates conjugate verbs. Personally, a workbook like this would have been a lifesaver for me, because hiding the sexy romance epics I was writing was difficult, though not as difficult as explaining to my teacher what I knew about clandestine Elvish trysts. AHEM!

When I was an English teacher, I used to doggedly dig into online resources or write my own prompts for bellwork or sub plans, despite how absolutely drained I was at the end of every day, and would have paid top dollar for someone— ANYONE—to hand me a workbook I could get excited about.

Use these prompts for bellwork. For extension activities to challenge the kid who's at least three grade levels above the rest of the class. For sub assignments you don't have to grade the next day. For homework when they need the extra practice. Use it any way you see fit.

Mostly, I hope this workbook gives you a no-fuss way to let your students' creativity run bananas through the aisles. Or, if you're not a teacher and are largely confused why I'm addressing you as one, use it to let your own creativity spark and set the entire world ablaze.

Cheers!

Kelly

FICTION

20 STORY STARTERS
CONTINUE WRITING THE SCENE.

WHAT'S A SCENE?

Picture an actor whispering a dramatic line about the villain getting away. The actor's perfectly shaped eyebrow is raised. Her love interest (a tall, broody pirate perhaps?) is standing nearby, staring moodily into the distance, wondering what our leading lady will do next. After they climb aboard her motorcycle and roar away into the distance, the director yells, "Cut!" and this scene is over. In short, a scene is simply a small part of a larger story. A single puzzle piece.

In the upcoming pages, you'll receive the first lines of a scene and you'll continue the story.

HOW DO I WRITE IT?

- **Stay small.** These miniature tales should be set in a particular place at a particular time with one or two characters. Think small and deep rather than broad and shallow.
- **Add conflict.** Most of the story starters give you a problem. Make it central to the scene and you'll add more drama.
- **Get sensory.** Add at least one sound, scent, taste, feeling, or sight to bring the scene to life.
- **Be emotional.** A scene is nothing without emotion. If you can't think of an emotion to give to your character, look up the Junto Institute's Emotion Wheel and choose one!

HOW DO I FINISH IT?

You don't have to. These are practice writing exercises and sometimes it's tough to find a tidy ending. Just focus on writing. If you *do*, however, want to end your scene well, then fix the conflict the main character faces. Maybe they find a home for the bird that's landed in their hand. Maybe they push the arrow through their shoulder and crawl away toward help. Maybe they sit in silence instead of screaming if a single noise means trouble.

TIP: UNDERSTANDING POV

Each story starter gives you the point of view (POV) or the angle from which the story is told.

It'll usually be in **1st person**, where the main character narrates their own story (I am cool and do cool things) or **3rd person**, where an outside observer tells the story (She/he/they were extremely cool).

Don't change the narrator in the same scene or you'll be committing the dreaded POV shift. *shudders*

STORY STARTERS

EXAMPLE

Sample Story Starter: Don't judge me. The blue delivery van is open, and on. What do you expect me to do? I mean, it's just sitting there in front of...

Sample Response:
...So Fresh, So Clean Laundromat and Dry Cleaners with the keys still in the ignition. People have a lot of faith in humanity, I swear.

Energy crackles through my nervous system and I do a quick lookie-loo over my shoulder. There's a couple of guys smoking on the curb. One laughs and gives me an interested eyebrow. I drop to a knee behind the van, pretend to tie my shoelace because I am exactly as slick as that. Eventually, he turns back to his buddy. There's a homeless lady pushing a Meijer shopping cart in front of the abandoned gas station. She's got nervous energy coming off of her in waves, so it seems she doesn't care about anything, least of all me. There are just a few cars on the road, bass rattling my fillings as they cruise by, their heavy *dunn, dunn, dunnnnn* fading away as they do. Besides the dude, nobody seems to care, even the owner of this van.

I can hear you now: *Stop. You can still walk away from this.*

From me to you, kindly shut up. Opportunities don't just present themselves like this every day. Trust me, I've been paying attention.

Tugging my baseball cap low over my face, blocking out what security cams can see, I slide up the driver's side of the van under the windows, and slip my work gloves over my fingers. No fingerprints, no crime. A deep breath in and out. My hand snakes up to the handle and I ease the door open and wait for a scream.

Nothing.

I slither through the crack I've made in the door. I'm sliding into the driver's seat, head down, hair tucked in my hat, bill shielding my face and hear the dude across the street yell, "Hey!"

Crap. Before anyone else notices, I jam it in reverse, three point turn it, then spin toward the road.

The man holds a hand over his eyes and jogs across the street, cigarette hanging out of loose lips. "Yo!" he yells around the smoke. You'd think he had something better to do than be a hero, but apparently not.

My breath coming quick, nerves firing, I screech out onto the road before anyone else notices what I'm doing. The man yells something else at me, an arm raised, but I'm gone. He grows smaller in my rear-view mirror, and eventually, drops his arm.

STORY STARTERS

CONTINUE WRITING THE SCENE.

1. Considering all the ways this morning went right, it's weird to be sitting here with an arrow through my shoulder. On my left is a crumpled sheet of paper. On my right, my dead phone lies useless. I grab...

_____

_____

_____

_____

_____

_____

_____

_____

_____

_____

_____

_____

_____

_____

_____

_____

_____

_____

_____

_____

_____

_____

_____

STORY STARTERS

CONTINUE WRITING THE SCENE.

2. When I looked at the photos of the missing kid, they were kinda hard to believe because the pictures were of me. And I wasn't missing. Immediately, I picked up the phone to text her, but before I could...

_____

_____

_____

_____

_____

_____

_____

_____

_____

_____

_____

_____

_____

_____

_____

_____

_____

_____

_____

_____

_____

_____

_____

STORY STARTERS

CONTINUE WRITING THE SCENE.

3. *She needs to do it*, Rodrigo thought to himself as he watched Andrea, trembling, perched behind the dumpster. The man in the white baseball cap strolled by, completely oblivious. Andrea's hand tightened around the knife, and without warning, she...

_____

_____

_____

_____

_____

_____

_____

_____

_____

_____

_____

_____

_____

_____

_____

_____

_____

_____

_____

_____

_____

_____

_____

_____

_____

STORY STARTERS
CONTINUE WRITING THE SCENE.

4. I stand in the remains of the tent, shocked, staring at the carnage. There's blood everywhere. A body is broken like a rag doll in the corner. Tony? I swallow around a lump in my throat, and take a cautious step toward the figure. When I touch his shoulder, he...

_____

_____

_____

_____

_____

_____

_____

_____

_____

_____

_____

_____

_____

_____

_____

_____

_____

_____

_____

_____

_____

STORY STARTERS

CONTINUE WRITING THE SCENE.

5. I groan, chasing after the scraggly-haired woman who just stole my wallet. I collide with a magazine rack and glossy pages scatter as the rack crashes into the front window. A spiderweb crack blooms. *Great.* Cringing at the mess, I bolt into the parking lot and...

_____

_____

_____

_____

_____

_____

_____

_____

_____

_____

_____

_____

_____

_____

_____

_____

_____

_____

_____

_____

_____

_____

_____

_____

STORY STARTERS

CONTINUE WRITING THE SCENE.

6. Ache blooms in my chest. Taylor knows how much I wanted Mason to like me. Had basically forced me to go through and like all his pictures on social media after my mom had finally gotten me a phone. And now she's suddenly going out with him? I grit my teeth and...

_____

_____

_____

_____

_____

_____

_____

_____

_____

_____

_____

_____

_____

_____

_____

_____

_____

_____

_____

_____

_____

_____

STORY STARTERS

CONTINUE WRITING THE SCENE.

7. Jess, tucking a flower into Finn's hair, raises her soft hazel eyes to his, expecting warmth or a hint of a smile at the corners of his lips. But no. Finn's eyes are sharp like the blades he wears on his hips. When he speaks, his voice is deadly calm and...

_____

_____

_____

_____

_____

_____

_____

_____

_____

_____

_____

_____

_____

_____

_____

_____

_____

_____

_____

_____

_____

_____

_____

_____

STORY STARTERS

CONTINUE WRITING THE SCENE.

8. When the firekeepers came for Aven, she knew the first thing they'd do—perform the ritual born from a century of lifetimes. But she also knew a secret that that they didn't and it was buried deep in her satin pocket, waiting for her to...

_____

_____

_____

_____

_____

_____

_____

_____

_____

_____

_____

_____

_____

_____

_____

_____

_____

_____

_____

_____

_____

_____

_____

STORY STARTERS

CONTINUE WRITING THE SCENE.

9. Kansas wouldn't have been all that bad if Ryan weren't currently stuffed in the trunk of a Toyota Corolla, mouth gagged, hands bound, headed west. He'd only stopped for a drink. One lousy drink and a game of pool, but that was *it,* and now he's clunking around like a spare tire headed toward...

_____

_____

_____

_____

_____

_____

_____

_____

_____

_____

_____

_____

_____

_____

_____

_____

_____

_____

_____

_____

_____

_____

_____

STORY STARTERS

CONTINUE WRITING THE SCENE.

10. Squished between a 6'3" football player and some lady talking into her collar, seat B in row 26 feels even smaller than it is, especially for a girl like me. I fix my headphones, wishing that Stella was here because she'd...

_____

_____

_____

_____

_____

_____

_____

_____

_____

_____

_____

_____

_____

_____

_____

_____

_____

_____

_____

_____

_____

_____

STORY STARTERS

CONTINUE WRITING THE SCENE.

11. Cass, breathing heavily, his mask on the deck, sat there with the stupid thing in his bleeding palm. It looked like a tiny statue, maybe a relic, but the way it was changing color made him believe...

_____

_____

_____

_____

_____

_____

_____

_____

_____

_____

_____

_____

_____

_____

_____

_____

_____

_____

_____

_____

_____

_____

_____

STORY STARTERS

CONTINUE WRITING THE SCENE.

12. Tyler never wanted to die like this. When he'd thought about death before he actually died, it was always in an abstract way. He'd be old, lying in his bed, sick. Not crushed in a car crash, three days before prom. But the real problem was that he was still here, wandering the halls of his high school, watching Olivia get away with murder. Not for long, though. He...

_____

_____

_____

_____

_____

_____

_____

_____

_____

_____

_____

_____

_____

_____

_____

_____

_____

_____

_____

_____

_____

STORY STARTERS

CONTINUE WRITING THE SCENE.

13. Abruptly, her mind made up, she clutched her pack and leapt from the airplane, a scream catching in her throat before she could give herself away. *Alex,* she thought as she landed softly in the murkiness of a midnight field, two miles from the farm. If I can find him, then...

_____

_____

_____

_____

_____

_____

_____

_____

_____

_____

_____

_____

_____

_____

_____

_____

_____

_____

_____

_____

_____

STORY STARTERS

CONTINUE WRITING THE SCENE.

14. Death is the worst scent, and I know that from experience. Hard to avoid in my line of work. But this alleyway's odor is a close second, considering what's in the bin. Bile rising in my throat, I...

_____

_____

_____

_____

_____

_____

_____

_____

_____

_____

_____

_____

_____

_____

_____

_____

_____

_____

_____

_____

_____

_____

STORY STARTERS

CONTINUE WRITING THE SCENE.

15. Bodie's cloudy stare says he doesn't want to remember, but the dance is seared into Maria's brain like a star-shaped scar. She only went with him to Homecoming because he'd begged. It was so pitiful, she couldn't say no. But now, as they look at each other over their steaming cups of coffee, Maria knows they have to make a decision about what to do about the files they stole. She... _____

_____

_____

_____

_____

_____

_____

_____

_____

_____

_____

_____

_____

_____

_____

_____

_____

_____

_____

_____

_____

_____

_____

STORY STARTERS

CONTINUE WRITING THE SCENE.

16. Creaking open the heavy wooden door, I step inside the old cellar. The December cold hits me like a fist, but the sound that permeates the dampness chills me to my core. It's a rusty-hinged scream followed by a...

_____

_____

_____

_____

_____

_____

_____

_____

_____

_____

_____

_____

_____

_____

_____

_____

_____

_____

_____

_____

_____

STORY STARTERS

CONTINUE WRITING THE SCENE.

17. The song Esther sang in that crystal soprano filled Dominick's ears until he felt like he'd cry. He watched her standing there on the dais, chained to her duty as the kingdom they'd both grew up in crumbled behind her. Turning, he muscled his composure into something suitable for a soldier and grabbed...

_____

_____

_____

_____

_____

_____

_____

_____

_____

_____

_____

_____

_____

_____

_____

_____

_____

_____

_____

_____

_____

_____

_____

_____

STORY STARTERS

CONTINUE WRITING THE SCENE.

18. When the lilacs bloom and the river starts to flow after the thaw, Jasmine walks into the forest behind her cottage and pulls out the gift her father gave her when she was still a child. She holds it up to the light, inspecting it for cracks. But it's just as it used to be, though the magic that hums inside of it has changed. Now, it...

_____

_____

_____

_____

_____

_____

_____

_____

_____

_____

_____

_____

_____

_____

_____

_____

_____

_____

_____

_____

_____

_____

_____

_____

STORY STARTERS

CONTINUE WRITING THE SCENE.

19. Elizabeth was eighteen when they met her for the first time. The crowd was mesmerized by her glowing skin, and rich, umber eyes, but they weren't prepared for her snakes. *They never are* she mused as they rose seemingly from the air around her, poised to strike. Jaiden was the first to...

_____

_____

_____

_____

_____

_____

_____

_____

_____

_____

_____

_____

_____

_____

_____

_____

_____

_____

_____

_____

_____

_____

_____

_____

STORY STARTERS

CONTINUE WRITING THE SCENE.

20. I stare at the slump of his shoulders as he turns away from me. I've hurt him badly and can't fix it. My heart squeezes painfully, but I shove it down. It isn't important right now. Not after what I've done. The entire city has been reduced to rubble because...

_____

_____

_____

_____

_____

_____

_____

_____

_____

_____

_____

_____

_____

_____

_____

_____

_____

_____

_____

_____

_____

_____

_____

SCENE SETTERS

WRITE A SCENE GIVEN AN OBJECT, AN EMOTION, AND A SETTING.

For these scenes, you'll be given the above items to use, which means you'll have to whittle your thoughts down a little bit more than you did in the previous section.

WHY AN OBJECT?

Symbolism. The object you're given, whether it's a shattered glass, a rainbow-painted zebra or a pencil sketch of shamrocks, can mean more than what it is. A shattered glass can symbolize emotional brokenness or rage. A rainbow can symbolize promises or pride. A shamrock can symbolize luck or the lack thereof. You can create meaning with the object to build suggested conflict, foreshadow an event to come, or even shock your reader. Or, you can use it just as it is.

WHY AN EMOTION?

Challenge. Many writers choose one or two big emotions from which to tell their stories. They'll choose happiness or sadness, anger or fear. But the emotions you're given challenge you to go a little bit deeper and address nuanced feeling like disappointment, bitterness, or contentment. You know, the stuff that's harder to define.

WHY A SETTING?

Surprise. Every story takes place *somewhere*, so why does it always have to be in someone's car or kitchen? These settings, like a mannequin factory or the basket of a hot air balloon, give you room to surprise your own imagination so you can create something you might never have thought of before.

TIP: MASTERING VERB TENSE

Things that happen right now are written in **present tense.**
"I'm on a plane, squished next to a nun."
"Jeb waits by the door like the good dog he is."

Things that happened before are written in **past tense.**
"I was on a plane, squished next to a nun."
"Jeb waited by the door like the good dog he was."

Tell your story in either tense, but choose one
and stick to it unless your character is diving into
memories!

SCENE SETTERS

EXAMPLE

Sample Scene Setter:
Object: A ceiling fan spinning way too fast.
Emotion: Gloominess.
Setting: A living room crowded with autumn decorations.

Sample Response:
"I don't mean to be dramatic, but if I die in this house, it's because I was sacrificed to the gods of fall décor." I prop my new suitcase against the kitchen pantry door and drop my duffel on top.

My mom's sigh can probably be heard on the moon. "Morgan Montrose."

"What is she doing, though?" I cut the gloominess out of my voice, because I don't do emotions, but it's hard even for me, because look around. Fall has exploded e-v-e-r-y-w-h-e-r-e. Gold banners that say "Falling Leaves Festival" stretch across the sage green sofa in the living room. About a million pumpkin pie tins sit on the kitchen island. Flyers are piled on the floor by a giant dog dish, and a knot of orange organza is tumbleweeding across the living room in the breeze from a ceiling fan going 100 miles an hour.

"Dee runs the festival. You know that." She sighs again, tossing her cream woolen coat from Barneys on the only chair that's not holding a box of leafy vines. "But she said she'd clean it all up before we got here."

"Welp?" I hold my hand out toward the stairwell, which has festival t-shirts strewn up as far as I can see. "That worked out really well."

"Honey, remember the things we talked about, okay? You're gonna have to trust me." She bites her lip, stifling her ever-present overflowing emotions, the ones she ties around her throat like a scarf. As I shrug out of my hoodie, gloomy panic tries to crawl out of the box I shoved it in on the ride over. Aunt Dee commanded us an hour ago in her big boss voice to make ourselves at home when we arrived, but it's stuffy in here and the scent of pumpkin spice is thick enough to clog your nostrils. Guess I'll have to get used to it because Aunt Dee Dee Stott's cluttered house in Essex, Connecticut is where I live now.

Nope. Not where I live. Back up. Erasing that from my brain.

Aunt Dee Dee Stott's cluttered house in Essex Connecticut is where I'm staying for an extended vacation. Much better. Panic shoved back into the box. And bonus: I even get to hang out with their new dog. Not such a terrible trade-off for my dad, is it? *Is it?*

SCENE SETTERS

WRITE A SCENE GIVEN AN OBJECT, AN EMOTION, AND A SETTING.

1. Object: Shards of a broken champagne flute glinting in the sunlight.
Emotion: Disappointment.
Setting: A bustling mom-and-pop restaurant in a noisy city.

_____
_____
_____
_____
_____
_____
_____
_____
_____
_____
_____
_____
_____
_____
_____
_____
_____
_____
_____
_____
_____
_____
_____

SCENE SETTERS

WRITE A SCENE GIVEN AN OBJECT, AN EMOTION, AND A SETTING.

2. Object: A jar of cinnamon sticks.
Emotion: Dread.
Setting: The Sistine Chapel during a busy tour.

_____

_____

_____

_____

_____

_____

_____

_____

_____

_____

_____

_____

_____

_____

_____

_____

_____

_____

_____

_____

_____

_____

_____

SCENE SETTERS

WRITE A SCENE GIVEN AN OBJECT, AN EMOTION, AND A SETTING.

3. Object: A stack of Oreo cookies next to a tall glass of ice-cold milk.
Emotion: Insecurity.
Setting: A used car salesperson's office on a sweaty summer morning.

_____

_____

_____

_____

_____

_____

_____

_____

_____

_____

_____

_____

_____

_____

_____

_____

_____

_____

_____

_____

_____

_____

_____

_____

_____

_____

_____

SCENE SETTERS

WRITE A SCENE GIVEN AN OBJECT, AN EMOTION, AND A SETTING.

4. Object: A saxophone gleaming from a recent polish.
Emotion: Contentment.
Setting: A cemetery at midnight in a rural town.

_____

_____

_____

_____

_____

_____

_____

_____

_____

_____

_____

_____

_____

_____

_____

_____

_____

_____

_____

_____

_____

_____

_____

SCENE SETTERS

WRITE A SCENE GIVEN AN OBJECT, AN EMOTION, AND A SETTING.

5. Object: A zebra spray-painted with rainbow colors.
Emotion: Envy.
Setting: A newly refurbished lighthouse in Maine.

_____

_____

_____

_____

_____

_____

_____

_____

_____

_____

_____

_____

_____

_____

_____

_____

_____

_____

_____

_____

_____

_____

_____

_____

SCENE SETTERS

WRITE A SCENE GIVEN AN OBJECT, AN EMOTION, AND A SETTING.

6. Object: A pencil sketch of three shamrocks.
Emotion: Glee.
Setting: A mannequin factory run by a grizzled old man named Rich.

_____

_____

_____

_____

_____

_____

_____

_____

_____

_____

_____

_____

_____

_____

_____

_____

_____

_____

_____

_____

_____

SCENE SETTERS

WRITE A SCENE GIVEN AN OBJECT, AN EMOTION, AND A SETTING.

7. Object: A hot air balloon just starting to inflate.
Emotion: Shock.
Setting: The Grand Canyon at dusk.

SCENE SETTERS

WRITE A SCENE GIVEN AN OBJECT, AN EMOTION, AND A SETTING.

8. Object: A full set of acrylic nails painted blood red.
Emotion: Hopefulness.
Setting: Deep inside the darkness of a coal mine.

_____

_____

_____

_____

_____

_____

_____

_____

_____

_____

_____

_____

_____

_____

_____

_____

_____

_____

_____

_____

_____

_____

SCENE SETTERS

WRITE A SCENE GIVEN AN OBJECT, AN EMOTION, AND A SETTING.

9. Object: A green plastic clock with a ticking second hand.
Emotion: Revulsion.
Setting: A high school science lab at 5:00 in the morning.

SCENE SETTERS

WRITE A SCENE GIVEN AN OBJECT, AN EMOTION, AND A SETTING.

10. Object: A package of hamburger buns that expired four days ago.
Emotion: Pride.
Setting: A cornfield next to a scarecrow wearing a pale pink hat.

_____

_____

_____

_____

_____

_____

_____

_____

_____

_____

_____

_____

_____

_____

_____

_____

_____

_____

_____

_____

_____

_____

_____

SCENE SETTERS

WRITE A SCENE GIVEN AN OBJECT, AN EMOTION, AND A SETTING.

11. Object: A ripe lemon sliced into plump wedges.
Emotion: Delight.
Setting: A humid jungle filled with dripping vines.

_____

_____

_____

_____

_____

_____

_____

_____

_____

_____

_____

_____

_____

_____

_____

_____

_____

_____

_____

_____

_____

_____

_____

_____

_____

SCENE SETTERS

WRITE A SCENE GIVEN AN OBJECT, AN EMOTION, AND A SETTING.

12. Object: A purple Croc with a plastic number three in one of the holes.
Emotion: Longing.
Setting: A winding, dusty road on the hottest day of the year.

_____

_____

_____

_____

_____

_____

_____

_____

_____

_____

_____

_____

_____

_____

_____

_____

_____

_____

_____

_____

_____

_____

_____

SCENE SETTERS

WRITE A SCENE GIVEN AN OBJECT, AN EMOTION, AND A SETTING.

13. Object: A small pile of pinecones on a caramel colored table.
Emotion: Panic.
Setting: A pottery studio owned by four college friends.

_____

_____

_____

_____

_____

_____

_____

_____

_____

_____

_____

_____

_____

_____

_____

_____

_____

_____

_____

_____

_____

_____

_____

_____

SCENE SETTERS

WRITE A SCENE GIVEN AN OBJECT, AN EMOTION, AND A SETTING.

14. Object: A bobblehead figurine on the dashboard of a car.
Emotion: Desire.
Setting: A prison parking lot by the front door.

_____

_____

_____

_____

_____

_____

_____

_____

_____

_____

_____

_____

_____

_____

_____

_____

_____

_____

_____

_____

_____

_____

_____

SCENE SETTERS

WRITE A SCENE GIVEN AN OBJECT, AN EMOTION, AND A SETTING.

15. Object: A puppet with a decade of dust in its hair.
Emotion: Bitterness.
Setting: A middle school cafeteria when the bell rings for dismissal.

_____

_____

_____

_____

_____

_____

_____

_____

_____

_____

_____

_____

_____

_____

_____

_____

_____

_____

_____

_____

_____

_____

_____

SCENE SETTERS

WRITE A SCENE GIVEN AN OBJECT, AN EMOTION, AND A SETTING.

16. Object: A bottle with an X on the peeling, yellowed label.
Emotion: Helplessness.
Setting: A blood drive truck in a Walmart parking lot.

SCENE SETTERS

WRITE A SCENE GIVEN AN OBJECT, AN EMOTION, AND A SETTING.

17. Object: A ballerina tutu.
Emotion: Euphoria.
Setting: An exotic safari drive-through in a backwoods town.

_____

_____

_____

_____

_____

_____

_____

_____

_____

_____

_____

_____

_____

_____

_____

_____

_____

_____

_____

_____

_____

_____

_____

_____

SCENE SETTERS

WRITE A SCENE GIVEN AN OBJECT, AN EMOTION, AND A SETTING.

18. Object: A snarling chihuahua with missing teeth.
Emotion: Optimism.
Setting: A river barge during a karaoke cruise.

_____

_____

_____

_____

_____

_____

_____

_____

_____

_____

_____

_____

_____

_____

_____

_____

_____

_____

_____

_____

_____

_____

SCENE SETTERS

WRITE A SCENE GIVEN AN OBJECT, AN EMOTION, AND A SETTING.

19. Object: A long, jagged scar along someone's jawline.
Emotion: Affection.
Setting: A barber shop filled with men getting shaves and cuts.

SCENE SETTERS

WRITE A SCENE GIVEN AN OBJECT, AN EMOTION, AND A SETTING.

20. Object: A bucket of greasy, over-salted popcorn.
Emotion: Grief.
Setting: Inside the treehouse your grandpa built.

_____

_____

_____

_____

_____

_____

_____

_____

_____

_____

_____

_____

_____

_____

_____

_____

_____

_____

_____

_____

_____

_____

_____

DIALOGUE BUILDERS

FINISH WRITING THE DIALOGUE BETWEEN CHARACTERS.

WHAT'S DIALOGUE?

Dialogue is a fancy way of saying "conversation." It's simply the words people say to each other in a story. Dialogue is almost always set off by quotation marks, unless the writer is trying to make a poetic point. Be wary of this, though, because it can be confusing to the reader unless you're particularly skilled.

WHY DO WE NEED DIALOGUE?

You don't necessarily. But dialogue can do lots of things for your story including moving the plot forward, showing off the world in which the characters live, and demonstrating who the character is without having to spell it out. It's more effective, for instance, to show the horrible things some guy screeches at another after a heated soccer match than it is to explain that he was a jerk.

HOW DO I WRITE DIALOGUE?

- **Write what you know.** If you've ever had a conversation with another person, then you've created dialogue. If you have no idea where to start for these scenes, use a piece of a conversation you've already had as inspiration.
- **Create out loud.** Sometimes the words look great on the page, but when you read them back, you realize no one would ever talk like that. Say it out loud to double check.
- **Make it meaningful.** In real life, we say mundane things to each other all the time. You might have a half-hour conversation about milk, for crying out loud. In a story, you do need a little bit of that everyday stuff so your characters don't sound like robots, but if your character speaks, their words should do one of those important jobs like moving the plot forward.

TIP: USING DIALOGUE TAGS

The things characters say go inside quotation marks.
The words that show who said it go outside of the quotation marks.
"Listen, I just want to sleep," Erin said.
Jay folded his arms over his chest. "Don't we all."

You'll notice above that you can use both a dialogue tag like *Erin said* and an action like *Jay folded his arms over his chest* to indicate who is speaking. However, you should only use tags or actions if it's unclear who said what. Otherwise, just write the dialogue so you don't slow the story down.

DIALOGUE BUILDERS

EXAMPLE

Sample Dialogue Builder:

"Mother, I'm sorry for making you worry so much, but you have to know that I cannot marry Erez. He's a terrible person. I never knew how terrible he was before, but now I do."

She blinked at me in the soft light. "Has he done something to you?"

Sample Response:

Ignored me. Laughed at me. Mocked me. Denied me. Dismissed me. "Not outright. I mean, nothing you could hold him accountable for, but he's not kind."

"He's agreed to marry you. That's kinder than any other young man in Leharo would likely be." She shrugged a frail shoulder, her eyes bleak. "And I don't say this to hurt you because anyone—" her voice cracked. "Anyone would be lucky to get you. I know you don't like that he's been chosen for you, but that's the way of our city."

"But you weren't chosen for dad, were you? Tell me about your life outside of Leharo. What is that blanket you gave me? What clothes were you wearing? I know it wasn't like this. It couldn't have been."

She cleared her throat. "I came from another place, Adara. Yes. And the rules were so different you wouldn't even understand if I told you. But something happened and we had to leave, and we came here to Leharo looking for a simple life."

"You ended up with more than just a simple life." I folded my arms over my chest.

Her eyes filled. "We did. I won't deny it. We certainly did. The Purists are—confused, I think— about a lot of things. But we live here now and we must remain here and follow along. There are incredibly dangerous consequences you don't understand waiting for us if we do not."

"What kind of consequences, Mother? Like getting beaten for disobeying the rules?"

She closed her eyes. "That was never supposed to happen."

"Well, it is happening!" I stood up, pacing like a caged cabellus who hadn't been run in a month. "But it doesn't have to. Don't you see?"

"No, Adara. It doesn't, but you make it all worse. If you'd just go along—"

"I REFUSE!" I punched my fist into my palm. My bellow silenced the shrieking of the girls upstairs. A door slammed above me. "I resist. I will not be bent into something I am not because a group of men say I should be a certain way."

"Well, then you're in for heartache after heartache."

DIALOGUE BUILDERS

FINISH WRITING THE DIALOGUE BETWEEN CHARACTERS.

1. "I never wanted to hurt you." Alyssa sank lower into her chair, her chest boiling with emotions she didn't want to name.
"Then why did you do that?" Henry asked. "I needed that money!"

_____

_____

_____

_____

_____

_____

_____

_____

_____

_____

_____

_____

_____

_____

_____

_____

_____

_____

_____

_____

_____

_____

_____

DIALOGUE BUILDERS

FINISH WRITING THE DIALOGUE BETWEEN CHARACTERS.

2. "Are you on your way?" Shelby asks. "I've been waiting for an hour."
 "Don't rush me," her mom says irritably. "You know how it's been this past week."

_____

_____

_____

_____

_____

_____

_____

_____

_____

_____

_____

_____

_____

_____

_____

_____

_____

_____

_____

_____

_____

_____

DIALOGUE BUILDERS

FINISH WRITING THE DIALOGUE BETWEEN CHARACTERS.

3. "Jack never called me back." Austin laid his head against the seat rest.
"Have you considered that he doesn't like you?" Emma poked him gently in the arm.
"Obviously. That's the problem. Especially after last weekend."

_____

_____

_____

_____

_____

_____

_____

_____

_____

_____

_____

_____

_____

_____

_____

_____

_____

_____

_____

_____

_____

_____

_____

_____

DIALOGUE BUILDERS

FINISH WRITING THE DIALOGUE BETWEEN CHARACTERS.

4. "I wish you'd talk to me," I whisper into the phone. There's silence on the other end of the line, but I know she's there. "Simone, say something."
"Something." Her voice is hoarse.

_____

_____

_____

_____

_____

_____

_____

_____

_____

_____

_____

_____

_____

_____

_____

_____

_____

_____

_____

_____

_____

_____

DIALOGUE BUILDERS

FINISH WRITING THE DIALOGUE BETWEEN CHARACTERS.

5. "I'm not trying out for the lead because I'll never get it." Bea flung her books down.

"If you don't swing, you'll never get a hole in one," Hector said.

"If I hear one more golf analogy--" Bea let her voice trail off as Mr. Garcia headed their way from the theater. She swallowed, visibly upset. _____

_____

_____

_____

_____

_____

_____

_____

_____

_____

_____

_____

_____

_____

_____

_____

_____

_____

_____

_____

_____

_____

_____

_____

DIALOGUE BUILDERS

FINISH WRITING THE DIALOGUE BETWEEN CHARACTERS.

6. "But Dad--" Panic wraps itself around my throat as he crosses his arms over his chest.
"Whine all you want. I'm not changing my mind," he says.
 "But this means everything to me! Do you even get that?"

_____

_____

_____

_____

_____

_____

_____

_____

_____

_____

_____

_____

_____

_____

_____

_____

_____

_____

_____

_____

_____

_____

DIALOGUE BUILDERS
FINISH WRITING THE DIALOGUE BETWEEN CHARACTERS.

7. "You gotta work on your game, kid," JT shouted at me as he jogged off the field.
A thundercloud of anger rolled through my head. I wanted nothing more than to blast his cocky grin into the stratosphere, but he wasn't worth another suspension.
"Shut up," I said instead.
He smirked and my fist coiled.

_____

_____

_____

_____

_____

_____

_____

_____

_____

_____

_____

_____

_____

_____

_____

_____

_____

_____

_____

_____

_____

_____

_____

_____

DIALOGUE BUILDERS

FINISH WRITING THE DIALOGUE BETWEEN CHARACTERS.

8. "Then kiss me," Nyah demands, her full mouth in a pretty pout.
 "Now?" Desmond looks around the classroom, slowly filling with other seniors. "You serious?"
 Nyah's eyebrow raises in a challenge.

_____

_____

_____

_____

_____

_____

_____

_____

_____

_____

_____

_____

_____

_____

_____

_____

_____

_____

_____

_____

_____

DIALOGUE BUILDERS

FINISH WRITING THE DIALOGUE BETWEEN CHARACTERS.

9. "There's only one team between us and that championship and we're gonna stomp all over them!" The coach cried, her fist in the air.
Sarah met Inez's eyes and sighed. "She's the only one who believes it."
"You don't?" Inez asked. "With your record?"

_____

_____

_____

_____

_____

_____

_____

_____

_____

_____

_____

_____

_____

_____

_____

_____

_____

_____

_____

_____

_____

_____

_____

_____

DIALOGUE BUILDERS

FINISH WRITING THE DIALOGUE BETWEEN CHARACTERS.

10. "I'm not driving out into the park with a shovel. We don't even own a shovel," I huff.
"So, borrow one from your neighbor. He probably has one, right?" Lisette asks.
"People would think I was a serial killer out there trying to bury bodies," I groan.

_____

_____

_____

_____

_____

_____

_____

_____

_____

_____

_____

_____

_____

_____

_____

_____

_____

_____

_____

_____

_____

_____

DIALOGUE BUILDERS

FINISH WRITING THE DIALOGUE BETWEEN CHARACTERS.

11. "I'm going to find her, bludgeon her with a large rock, and then throw her over a cliff." Camilla stared at me with eyes hard like stones.

"What did Anya ever do to you?" I ask, though I don't want to know. Not really.

_____

_____

_____

_____

_____

_____

_____

_____

_____

_____

_____

_____

_____

_____

_____

_____

_____

_____

_____

_____

_____

_____

_____

DIALOGUE BUILDERS

FINISH WRITING THE DIALOGUE BETWEEN CHARACTERS.

12. "You don't need to worry, you know." Kizzie pops the bite into her mouth and chews.
 "What do you mean? Of course, I need to worry," Josie splutters.
 "Nah. Our revenge is coming. I promise you that."

_____

_____

_____

_____

_____

_____

_____

_____

_____

_____

_____

_____

_____

_____

_____

_____

_____

_____

_____

_____

_____

DIALOGUE BUILDERS

FINISH WRITING THE DIALOGUE BETWEEN CHARACTERS.

13. "Where were you last night?" Francine's mom asked her.
Dancing, kissing, drinking, crying. "I stayed with a friend."

_____

_____

_____

_____

_____

_____

_____

_____

_____

_____

_____

_____

_____

_____

_____

_____

_____

_____

_____

_____

_____

_____

_____

DIALOGUE BUILDERS

FINISH WRITING THE DIALOGUE BETWEEN CHARACTERS.

14. "You sad?" Zander asks Tiana.

"Yeah. Just a sucky day. People are idiots. Everyone in my class is an idiot. A friend who was supposed to be a friend is spreading rumors about me."

Zander nudges her gently. "Wanna do something about it?"

_____

_____

_____

_____

_____

_____

_____

_____

_____

_____

_____

_____

_____

_____

_____

_____

_____

_____

_____

_____

_____

_____

_____

DIALOGUE BUILDERS

FINISH WRITING THE DIALOGUE BETWEEN CHARACTERS.

15. "Sydney?" My mom called from downstairs. There was a clunk as she kicked her work heels off into the foyer.

"Yeah?" I croaked, smacking some color into my cheeks. *Act sick,* I commanded myself as her soft steps padded up the carpeted stairs. *She can't know.*

_____

_____

_____

_____

_____

_____

_____

_____

_____

_____

_____

_____

_____

_____

_____

_____

_____

_____

_____

_____

_____

_____

_____

_____

DIALOGUE BUILDERS

FINISH WRITING THE DIALOGUE BETWEEN CHARACTERS.

16. "You coming to Abuelita's tonight?" Talia asks Ms. Barton.
 Our teacher waves her off. "The only thing I want to do is curl up with a trashy romance novel and a glass of Chardonnay. I've been here since 6:30 this morning."
 Talia looks at me. "How about you?"

_____

_____

_____

_____

_____

_____

_____

_____

_____

_____

_____

_____

_____

_____

_____

_____

_____

_____

_____

_____

_____

_____

DIALOGUE BUILDERS

FINISH WRITING THE DIALOGUE BETWEEN CHARACTERS.

17. "Breathe through the pain." Eris held the fire between his palms, pressing, pressing.
"But I'm no match for it--" I cried.
"You are if you use your gift," he countered, sweat beading on his brow.

_____

_____

_____

_____

_____

_____

_____

_____

_____

_____

_____

_____

_____

_____

_____

_____

_____

_____

_____

_____

_____

_____

DIALOGUE BUILDERS

FINISH WRITING THE DIALOGUE BETWEEN CHARACTERS.

18. "Where is everyone?" Sophie asks me as she takes off her coat and hooks it on the rack by the door.

"Gone. Because of what you did, obviously." I stare at her. This is *her* fault. If it weren't for that whole thing with Taylor, the entire house would be pulsing with people.

_____

_____

_____

_____

_____

_____

_____

_____

_____

_____

_____

_____

_____

_____

_____

_____

_____

_____

_____

_____

_____

_____

DIALOGUE BUILDERS

FINISH WRITING THE DIALOGUE BETWEEN CHARACTERS.

19. "Is that empty?" the lady asked.
I blinked at the lone register to my left. "I mean, it clearly is. The drawer is wide open."
Her eyes darted to my hand still holding the money. "Gimme it."

_____

_____

_____

_____

_____

_____

_____

_____

_____

_____

_____

_____

_____

_____

_____

_____

_____

_____

_____

_____

_____

_____

DIALOGUE BUILDERS

FINISH WRITING THE DIALOGUE BETWEEN CHARACTERS.

20. "You need a raise," I tell my mom.

Her eyes flash. "Mae pays me everything she can. But it's a fast food job. You make more than me *and* Dion right now."

"Not anymore." I stuff my hands into my pockets and stare at the floor.

_____

_____

_____

_____

_____

_____

_____

_____

_____

_____

_____

_____

_____

_____

_____

_____

_____

_____

_____

_____

_____

NONFICTION

PERSONAL QUERIES

ANSWER QUESTIONS ABOUT YOUR OWN EXPERIENCES.

WHY WRITE ABOUT MYSELF?

There are close to a zillion reasons to write about your own life, but one of the big ones is getting to know yourself. Some people never look inward, but diving into your own experiences can shine a flashlight on who you are deep inside where no one else can see.

That knowledge is helpful for a variety of things:
- explaining your beliefs without letting your emotions run off into the wild blue yonder
- writing an essay that can get you into college
- talking to a hiring manager on your first professional job interview
- communicating with partners, parents, loved ones, children, friends, and coworkers
- questioning your beliefs, thoughts, actions, biases, logic, and choices you make along the journey of life

WHAT'S THE BEST WAY TO ANSWER THESE QUESTIONS?

With honesty. That's the short answer. Take the opportunity in these few moments to truly consider your responses to the questions and pull a story out of yourself that explains. You can leave second-guessing and doubt at the door. Your gut will tell you what to write if you're willing to listen!

TIP: CHANGING SENTENCE LENGTH

Challenge yourself in this section to use a variety of sentence lengths and structures. Go short. Intentional fragments? Yes please! Explore medium length sentences with just a clause or two. Try longer, more complex sentences that give you space to add context, suggestion, inspiration, and—if the mood strikes—sensory or poetic language.
The variety adds rhythm to your writing, which is the beating heart of human communication.

PERSONAL QUERIES

EXAMPLE

Sample Personal Query: What is an accomplishment, event, or realization that sparked a period of personal growth and a new understanding of yourself?

Sample Response:
The first thing that hit me about Mrs. Jackson's house was the stuffiness and the smell of old broccoli rotting in the sink. I held back a gag as I kicked off my shoes. When I saw the older lady sitting in her wheelchair, I tried not to gasp. She couldn't have weighed more than ninety pounds. The cancer had whittled her down to bones. *I'm not strong enough for this*, I thought.

But I got busy anyway, despite my utter lack of courage. As I did the chores my mom had volunteered me to do—sweep the floors, feed the cats, wash the dishes—I worried that I wasn't doing things right. I worried about being there and not spending enough time on my AP Calculus homework. While the sound of Judge Judy droned in the background, I spooned stinky cat food onto plates, wishing I was home safe, practicing piano, instead of feeding cats who seemed angry I was there. An hour later, when I said goodbye and closed the door, I breathed in the scent of clean air and realized I should have opened a window.

It gave me a reason to go back.

I made it through the next day and the one after that, watching Mrs. Jackson in her red lipstick, determined to use the bathroom on her own. Determined to keep writing her memoir, even though she was only halfway done and six weeks away from dying according to the hospice nurses. We talked sometimes while I scrubbed the floor or put away groceries, and I learned that though she was in severe pain, she wore pretty, floral dresses because she didn't want to die in an old robe. She said she was afraid of death, but that she was going to face it head on like a prize fighter in a boxing ring. She feigned a one-two punch with her scrawny arms and I laughed.

The more I worked and the more she insisted on doing things for herself despite growing weaker, the less afraid I became of problems in my life. I might not get an A in AP Calculus, and that was okay. I might mess up my senior choir recital, and that was okay. Mrs. Jackson might not make it through December, and I wasn't sure I'd be okay about that, but I vowed to join her in the ring and face it head on, anyway.

The last day I worked in her house, when she couldn't get out of bed at all, she hugged me with all the strength in her baby bird arms. I tried not to cry, but she said to go ahead. Crying wasn't weakness; it was just a way for your system to wash itself clean. The last memory I have of her was of her small frame lying on the bed, a multicolor floral dress spread around her like a field of roses. She was so frail on the outside, but it didn't match who she was on the inside. She was tougher than anyone I'd ever met.

While I might have been helping Mrs. Jackson with her neglected housework, she was helping me learn the true meaning of courage. Courage isn't not being afraid; it's being afraid and doing it anyway. As I get older, I'll remember the courage Mrs. Jackson taught me each time I'm afraid to try something new. I'll be a person who's ready to give a one-two punch to life's challenges, just the way she taught me.

PERSONAL QUERIES

ANSWER QUESTIONS ABOUT YOUR OWN EXPERIENCES.

1. Will you explain an instance where you failed, faced a challenge, or handled a setback? How did it affect you, and what strengths did you unearth about yourself?

_____

_____

_____

_____

_____

_____

_____

_____

_____

_____

_____

_____

_____

_____

_____

_____

_____

_____

_____

_____

_____

PERSONAL QUERIES

ANSWER QUESTIONS ABOUT YOUR OWN EXPERIENCES.

2. If laughter is the best medicine, do you think we, as a society, are laughing enough? If not, will you describe a great remedy to heal us?

_____

_____

_____

_____

_____

_____

_____

_____

_____

_____

_____

_____

_____

_____

_____

_____

_____

_____

_____

_____

_____

_____

_____

PERSONAL QUERIES

ANSWER QUESTIONS ABOUT YOUR OWN EXPERIENCES.

3. Which song hits you right in the gut every time you listen to it? Who's the artist? What do you connect with the most? Consider the lyrics, the rhythm, the instruments, the melody and more.

_____

_____

_____

_____

_____

_____

_____

_____

_____

_____

_____

_____

_____

_____

_____

_____

_____

_____

_____

_____

_____

_____

PERSONAL QUERIES

ANSWER QUESTIONS ABOUT YOUR OWN EXPERIENCES.

4. Will you describe the very best parts of your personality? What sets you apart from your friends and family? In which ways are you happy with who you are?

_____

_____

_____

_____

_____

_____

_____

_____

_____

_____

_____

_____

_____

_____

_____

_____

_____

_____

_____

_____

_____

_____

_____

_____

PERSONAL QUERIES

ANSWER QUESTIONS ABOUT YOUR OWN EXPERIENCES.

5. Will you explain something that someone has done for you that has made you happy or thankful in a surprising way? How has this gratitude changed or inspired you?

_____

_____

_____

_____

_____

_____

_____

_____

_____

_____

_____

_____

_____

_____

_____

_____

_____

_____

_____

_____

_____

_____

_____

_____

_____

PERSONAL QUERIES

ANSWER QUESTIONS ABOUT YOUR OWN EXPERIENCES.

6. Have you ever been told you look like someone famous? If so, how did you react? Did you like the comparison? If you've never been told that, who do you think you resemble either physically, mentally, or emotionally?

_____

_____

_____

_____

_____

_____

_____

_____

_____

_____

_____

_____

_____

_____

_____

_____

_____

_____

_____

_____

_____

_____

_____

_____

PERSONAL QUERIES

ANSWER QUESTIONS ABOUT YOUR OWN EXPERIENCES.

7. If you wrote your memoir, what would the title be? On which personal conflict would you center your story? How is your future influenced by your past?

_____

_____

_____

_____

_____

_____

_____

_____

_____

_____

_____

_____

_____

_____

_____

_____

_____

_____

_____

_____

_____

_____

_____

_____

PERSONAL QUERIES

ANSWER QUESTIONS ABOUT YOUR OWN EXPERIENCES.

8. If you were to be responsible for a child right now, how would you parent differently than you were raised? Which parenting choices would you borrow from those who raised you?

_____

_____

_____

_____

_____

_____

_____

_____

_____

_____

_____

_____

_____

_____

_____

_____

_____

_____

_____

_____

_____

_____

_____

PERSONAL QUERIES

ANSWER QUESTIONS ABOUT YOUR OWN EXPERIENCES.

9. What are three characteristics of the best kind of leader? How could your personal strengths help you in leadership positions? Which areas do you still need to strengthen?

_____

_____

_____

_____

_____

_____

_____

_____

_____

_____

_____

_____

_____

_____

_____

_____

_____

_____

_____

_____

_____

_____

_____

PERSONAL QUERIES

ANSWER QUESTIONS ABOUT YOUR OWN EXPERIENCES.

10. Will you describe the last time you went out of your way to help someone? How did it make the other person feel? How did it make you feel about yourself?

_____

_____

_____

_____

_____

_____

_____

_____

_____

_____

_____

_____

_____

_____

_____

_____

_____

_____

_____

_____

_____

_____

_____

_____

PERSONAL QUERIES

ANSWER QUESTIONS ABOUT YOUR OWN EXPERIENCES.

11. Will you describe a topic or activity that's so engaging it makes you lose all track of time? Why does it captivate you? What emotions come up when you think about it?

_____

_____

_____

_____

_____

_____

_____

_____

_____

_____

_____

_____

_____

_____

_____

_____

_____

_____

_____

_____

_____

_____

_____

_____

PERSONAL QUERIES

ANSWER QUESTIONS ABOUT YOUR OWN EXPERIENCES.

12. If there were no obstacles in your path—physical, financial, or otherwise—what would you choose to do for your profession as an adult? How do your current activities support or detract from your future goals?

_____

_____

_____

_____

_____

_____

_____

_____

_____

_____

_____

_____

_____

_____

_____

_____

_____

_____

_____

_____

_____

_____

_____

PERSONAL QUERIES

ANSWER QUESTIONS ABOUT YOUR OWN EXPERIENCES.

13. Will you describe the last time you had a sleepless or restless night? Were you awake by choice? If you tried to get yourself back to sleep, what did you do? If you were awake by choice, what kept you up? What thoughts were running through your head?

_____

_____

_____

_____

_____

_____

_____

_____

_____

_____

_____

_____

_____

_____

_____

_____

_____

_____

_____

_____

_____

PERSONAL QUERIES

ANSWER QUESTIONS ABOUT YOUR OWN EXPERIENCES.

14. If you could make one change that would help the world, what would it be? Describe the positive impacts of your decision. Consider the unintended consequences too.

_____

_____

_____

_____

_____

_____

_____

_____

_____

_____

_____

_____

_____

_____

_____

_____

_____

_____

_____

_____

_____

_____

_____

_____

_____

PERSONAL QUERIES

ANSWER QUESTIONS ABOUT YOUR OWN EXPERIENCES.

15. If you could give each person in the world the same gift, what would you give them? Why would you choose that and what would the response be from the recipients?

_____

_____

_____

_____

_____

_____

_____

_____

_____

_____

_____

_____

_____

_____

_____

_____

_____

_____

_____

_____

_____

_____

PERSONAL QUERIES

ANSWER QUESTIONS ABOUT YOUR OWN EXPERIENCES.

16. Will you describe a time you challenged a long-held idea or belief? What led to the challenge and how did it turn out?

_____

_____

_____

_____

_____

_____

_____

_____

_____

_____

_____

_____

_____

_____

_____

_____

_____

_____

_____

_____

_____

_____

_____

_____

PERSONAL QUERIES

ANSWER QUESTIONS ABOUT YOUR OWN EXPERIENCES.

17. What are five things you can do today to be happier than you are right now? Why would they help? If you're already bursting with joy, what are five things you could do to make someone else happier today?

_____

_____

_____

_____

_____

_____

_____

_____

_____

_____

_____

_____

_____

_____

_____

_____

_____

_____

_____

_____

_____

_____

_____

_____

PERSONAL QUERIES

ANSWER QUESTIONS ABOUT YOUR OWN EXPERIENCES.

18. Think about the best scent in the world. Describe it. Why do you like it? What or who does it remind you of? Would it smell as good to you if you experienced it in a different context?

_____

_____

_____

_____

_____

_____

_____

_____

_____

_____

_____

_____

_____

_____

_____

_____

_____

_____

_____

_____

_____

_____

PERSONAL QUERIES

ANSWER QUESTIONS ABOUT YOUR OWN EXPERIENCES.

19. What is a societal norm that you think needs to change? What would happen to our society if it did? What would happen to *you* if it changed?

_____

_____

_____

_____

_____

_____

_____

_____

_____

_____

_____

_____

_____

_____

_____

_____

_____

_____

_____

_____

_____

_____

_____

PERSONAL QUERIES

ANSWER QUESTIONS ABOUT YOUR OWN EXPERIENCES.

20. Will you describe the best day of your life in your future? Who is there? What are you doing? Where do you go? Why does it fill you with joy or contentment?

_____

_____

_____

_____

_____

_____

_____

_____

_____

_____

_____

_____

_____

_____

_____

_____

_____

_____

_____

_____

_____

_____

OPINION GRABBERS

EXPLAIN YOUR OPINION ABOUT THE GIVEN FACTUAL STATEMENT.

WHY WRITE ABOUT MY OPINION?

Have you ever had a great solution for a complex problem and then just...couldn't tell anyone? Whether it was fear of failure or a lack of support from others, *something* held you back.

Some people need practice sharing their thoughts, opinions, and solutions. Doing so in a thoughtful, logical way can help you better express yourself. Believe it or not, one day someone will ask for your opinion on finding better financial streams for the second fiscal quarter or might need your solution for the failing hydroponic farming stations. Will you be ready? Practicing now when the stakes are low will help make sure you know how to speak up when the stakes are a little bit higher.

WHAT IF I DON'T KNOW ANYTHING ABOUT THE TOPIC?

It can be tough to form an opinion without a knowledge base. If you come across a topic in this section that's beyond your experience, you have a couple of options:

- **Google it.** Yes, you can use your search skills to find out what experts in the field think before you form an opinion. Read up on it for a few minutes, finding differing opinions so you can see the range of ideas about the topic. Then offer your two cents.
- **Write about a related topic.** So maybe you don't have any idea about studying bowhead whales to benefit humankind, but you do have very strong opinions about cage-diving with sharks. Write about that instead. No harm, no foul.

TIP: CITING RESEARCH

These writing exercises are not designed to be research projects. As such, citing sources isn't required.

However, if you do come across a great source and want to give credit where credit is due, an easy way to do that is with an *informal citation* like this:

According to Sheryl Sandberg, founder of LeanIn.org, "Leaders should strive for authenticity over perfection."

OPINION GRABBERS

EXAMPLE

Sample Opinion Grabber: A study of more than 1,000 companies conducted by LeanIn.org and McKinsey and Company reveals that gender diversity is important for the bottom line in business. Companies with more gender diversity in executive positions had a 39% greater likelihood of financial outperformance than those with less gender diversity. *How could a company use this information to boost its profits?*

Sample Response:

This study shows that having gender diversity in top jobs is good for business across the board. Companies that want to increase their profitability should be making every effort to hire and promote more women into leadership roles since, according to the S&P 100, men still hold most of the executive positions.

Some people believe that trying to include a diverse gender pool means excluding men from roles that they've earned for themselves, but that's not what it means at all. Getting to maximum profitability for any company means actively recruiting a gender-diverse pool of talent so you can hire the best person for the job regardless of their gender, not because of it. It means giving everyone a fair chance to lead and share ideas. It means offering training, mentorship, and support for women who might not have anyone pulling for them from the top.

And it makes sense, too. I can see the difference in class when we have to work together on projects. When people with different experiences get together on a project, the project is way more creative, and the group comes up with better solutions than when people who all think the same way work together.

It really isn't about being fair for fair's sake; it's about being smart for business. If you want your company to make more money—which impacts everyone from shareholders to customers—it makes sense to follow the statistics that show where profitability comes from. Gender-diversity is one factor that contributes to that.

OPINION GRABBERS

EXPLAIN YOUR OPINION ABOUT THE GIVEN FACTUAL STATEMENT.

1. Before the Pregnancy Discrimination Act of 1978, a person in the U.S. could be fired if they were pregnant. This act ensured that employers could not deny job opportunities to those who were, or might become, pregnant. Naysayers argue that protecting these rights creates more work for those who do not take parental leave. *How could a workplace address vacancies created by those who take parental leave?*

_____

_____

_____

_____

_____

_____

_____

_____

_____

_____

_____

_____

_____

_____

_____

_____

_____

_____

_____

_____

_____

_____

OPINION GRABBERS

EXPLAIN YOUR OPINION ABOUT THE GIVEN FACTUAL STATEMENT.

2. According to CDC and NHTSA data, approximately 34 people die each day from alcohol-impaired driving crashes. That's one approximately every 42 minutes. *How can we solve the problem of drunk driving?*

_____

_____

_____

_____

_____

_____

_____

_____

_____

_____

_____

_____

_____

_____

_____

_____

_____

_____

_____

_____

_____

_____

_____

_____

OPINION GRABBERS

EXPLAIN YOUR OPINION ABOUT THE GIVEN FACTUAL STATEMENT.

3. On Easter Island (Rapa Nui), a territory of Chile in the southeastern Pacific, there are nearly 900 Moai or statues which average 13 feet in height and weigh 14 tons. They were built by Rapa Nui people between 1100 and 1650 AD to honor chieftains or other people. *How do you imagine these heavy statues were placed so carefully around the island?*

_____

_____

_____

_____

_____

_____

_____

_____

_____

_____

_____

_____

_____

_____

_____

_____

_____

_____

_____

_____

_____

_____

_____

_____

OPINION GRABBERS

EXPLAIN YOUR OPINION ABOUT THE GIVEN FACTUAL STATEMENT.

4. The Environmental Protection Agency states that each person in the U.S. generates about 4.9 pounds of trash per day. *What can you do to reduce your own impact this week?*

_____

_____

_____

_____

_____

_____

_____

_____

_____

_____

_____

_____

_____

_____

_____

_____

_____

_____

_____

_____

_____

_____

_____

OPINION GRABBERS

EXPLAIN YOUR OPINION ABOUT THE GIVEN FACTUAL STATEMENT.

5. Bowhead whales, which live in the Arctic year round, can live more than 200 years, making them the longest-living mammals in the world. *Should they be studied for the benefit of human longevity?*

_____

_____

_____

_____

_____

_____

_____

_____

_____

_____

_____

_____

_____

_____

_____

_____

_____

_____

_____

_____

_____

_____

OPINION GRABBERS

EXPLAIN YOUR OPINION ABOUT THE GIVEN FACTUAL STATEMENT.

6. From 1692 - 1693, more than 200 people were accused of witchcraft in Salem, Massachusetts. Nineteen people were hanged to death for the crime, and the trials to convict them became known as the Salem Witch Trials. *Is it ever right for a governmental body to take someone's life? Why or why not?*

OPINION GRABBERS

EXPLAIN YOUR OPINION ABOUT THE GIVEN FACTUAL STATEMENT.

7. Nauru, an island country in the southwestern Pacific Ocean, is only 8.1 square miles, making it the third smallest country in the world behind Monaco and Vatican City. *Would you want to live in a country of this size? Why or why not?*

_____

_____

_____

_____

_____

_____

_____

_____

_____

_____

_____

_____

_____

_____

_____

_____

_____

_____

_____

_____

_____

_____

OPINION GRABBERS

EXPLAIN YOUR OPINION ABOUT THE GIVEN FACTUAL STATEMENT.

8. "The Wreck of the Titan: Or, Futility" was a novella by Morgan Robertson that seemed to predict the sinking of the Titanic. Written in 1898, fourteen years before the Titanic sailed, the story follows ocean liner Titan, which strikes an iceberg in the Atlantic and sinks. Eerily similar details include the month the boats sink (April) and the side upon which they're hit (starboard). *Do you believe there are people who can predict the future?*

_____

_____

_____

_____

_____

_____

_____

_____

_____

_____

_____

_____

_____

_____

_____

_____

_____

_____

_____

_____

_____

_____

_____

OPINION GRABBERS

EXPLAIN YOUR OPINION ABOUT THE GIVEN FACTUAL STATEMENT.

9. Of the approximately 550,000 NCAA student athletes, fewer than 2 percent will go pro. *Is it worth pushing yourself hard in a sport throughout your childhood when you may never be a professional?*

_____

_____

_____

_____

_____

_____

_____

_____

_____

_____

_____

_____

_____

_____

_____

_____

_____

_____

_____

_____

_____

_____

_____

OPINION GRABBERS

EXPLAIN YOUR OPINION ABOUT THE GIVEN FACTUAL STATEMENT.

10. The University of Bologna in Italy is older than the Aztecs. The school was founded in 1088. The Aztecs, who likely developed from nomadic tribes, didn't settle in Mesoamerica until the 1200s. *Is it surprising that a university is older than an ancient civilization? Why or why not?*

OPINION GRABBERS

EXPLAIN YOUR OPINION ABOUT THE GIVEN FACTUAL STATEMENT.

11. The original iPhone, introduced in 2007, was called "a beautiful and breakthrough handheld computer" by the *Wall Street Journal. What fact about cell phones today would shock people in 2007?*

_____

_____

_____

_____

_____

_____

_____

_____

_____

_____

_____

_____

_____

_____

_____

_____

_____

_____

_____

_____

_____

_____

OPINION GRABBERS

EXPLAIN YOUR OPINION ABOUT THE GIVEN FACTUAL STATEMENT.

12. Blood donations are vital to many people's survival. To encourage more people to donate , Sahlgrenska University Hospital in Gothenburg, Sweden, sends a text to donors when their blood has been given to someone in need. *Would this entice you to donate blood? Why or why not?*

_____

_____

_____

_____

_____

_____

_____

_____

_____

_____

_____

_____

_____

_____

_____

_____

_____

_____

_____

_____

_____

_____

_____

OPINION GRABBERS

EXPLAIN YOUR OPINION ABOUT THE GIVEN FACTUAL STATEMENT.

13. Inventor Fredric Baur came up with the design for the Pringles can in 1966. When he died in 2008, his ashes were buried in one of the cans per his request. *How do you feel about non-traditional burials?*

_____

_____

_____

_____

_____

_____

_____

_____

_____

_____

_____

_____

_____

_____

_____

_____

_____

_____

_____

_____

_____

_____

OPINION GRABBERS

EXPLAIN YOUR OPINION ABOUT THE GIVEN FACTUAL STATEMENT.

14. New Mexico's Department of Transportation added rumble strips to a quarter-mile stretch of Route 66 between Albuquerque and Tijeras that play "America the Beautiful" if you're driving 45 mph over them. *What other creative edits do people make to ordinary things that improve them?*

_____

_____

_____

_____

_____

_____

_____

_____

_____

_____

_____

_____

_____

_____

_____

_____

_____

_____

_____

_____

_____

_____

_____

_____

OPINION GRABBERS

EXPLAIN YOUR OPINION ABOUT THE GIVEN FACTUAL STATEMENT.

15. Jane C. Wright was a pioneering cancer research scientist and surgeon noted for her contributions to the field of chemotherapy. Her paternal grandfather had been born into slavery, but became a doctor, starting a family history of physicians who changed the face of medicine. *What does it take for someone to overcome nearly insurmountable odds to create a legacy of greatness?*

_____

_____

_____

_____

_____

_____

_____

_____

_____

_____

_____

_____

_____

_____

_____

_____

_____

_____

_____

_____

_____

_____

_____

_____

OPINION GRABBERS

EXPLAIN YOUR OPINION ABOUT THE GIVEN FACTUAL STATEMENT.

16. In Ohio, if someone has a second DUI conviction or a first DUI conviction with a high blood alcohol content, they are required to use yellow license plates on their vehicles instead of white if they get their driving privileges back. *Do you think this is fair? Why or why not?*

_____

_____

_____

_____

_____

_____

_____

_____

_____

_____

_____

_____

_____

_____

_____

_____

_____

_____

_____

_____

_____

_____

_____

_____

OPINION GRABBERS

EXPLAIN YOUR OPINION ABOUT THE GIVEN FACTUAL STATEMENT.

17. Kintsugi is the Japanese art form of mending broken pottery. Rather than throwing away a cracked dish, a kintsugi artist puts the pieces back together with lacquer mixed with powdered gold, creating a different look. *Does our society place value on broken things?*

_____

_____

_____

_____

_____

_____

_____

_____

_____

_____

_____

_____

_____

_____

_____

_____

_____

_____

_____

_____

_____

_____

OPINION GRABBERS

EXPLAIN YOUR OPINION ABOUT THE GIVEN FACTUAL STATEMENT.

18. Former NFL linebacker Myles Jack transitioned into a surprising and successful second career after football. After retiring in 2023, he became the co-owner of the Allen Americans, a professional hockey team, and later enlisted in the U.S. Army to pursue a lifelong passion for service. *Should everyone consider second or third career paths?*

_____

_____

_____

_____

_____

_____

_____

_____

_____

_____

_____

_____

_____

_____

_____

_____

_____

_____

_____

_____

_____

_____

_____

OPINION GRABBERS

EXPLAIN YOUR OPINION ABOUT THE GIVEN FACTUAL STATEMENT.

19. Malcolm Gladwell says in his book, *Outliers*, that it takes 10,000 hours (or approximately ten years) of practice to become an expert at something. *Does practice really make perfect?*

_____

_____

_____

_____

_____

_____

_____

_____

_____

_____

_____

_____

_____

_____

_____

_____

_____

_____

_____

_____

_____

_____

_____

OPINION GRABBERS

EXPLAIN YOUR OPINION ABOUT THE GIVEN FACTUAL STATEMENT.

20. George Eliot, one of the leading writers of the Victorian era, was a woman. She used a male pen name because women were not taken seriously in the mid-1800s and she wanted her books to be judged on their merit only. *In what ways does society place limits on people based on their assumed genders?*

_____

_____

_____

_____

_____

_____

_____

_____

_____

_____

_____

_____

_____

_____

_____

_____

_____

_____

_____

_____

_____

_____

_____

DEBATABLE TOPICS

CONSIDER TWO OR MORE SIDES OF A CONTROVERSIAL SUBJECT.

WHY SHOULD I ARGUE MY POINT?

Debating a topic might not make you popular at a party when everyone's trying to have a good time, but it could very well win you an argument, a prestigious law school acceptance, a career supporting underserved youth, or even a presidency. Debate does all sorts of nifty things like improving your:

- critical thinking skills
- creativity
- analytical ability
- confidence
- emotional maturity
- problem-solving ability

HOW DO YOU ARGUE YOUR POINT?

Arguing with a friend or family member is a little bit different than arguing a point when writing. In this section, try one of these methods:

- **Aristotelean:** Use this method if you have a strong opinion on one side. Start by stating your point, stating your opposition's point, and then providing all your evidence to prove your argument and disprove the opposition. You'll want to use logical reasoning, credibility, and emotion to sway your reader to your side.
- **Rogerian:** Use this method if you find both sides to be valid. Explain the validity of one side, then the other. After, explain a reasonable compromise that could unify or pacify both sides.

TIP: AVOIDING FALLACIES

Logical fallacies are lapses in logic that weaken a person's point when debating a topic. A popular one is called an **ad hominem** fallacy which means "against the man."

Let's say you're arguing against the death penalty, and you've quoted a politician so you can counter his point that it deters crime. You state that you can't trust him because he's a tax evader and terrible father, two things that have nothing to do with his opinion. That's a logical fallacy because you're not debating his idea; you're attacking him as a person.

Look up "logical fallacies" to see other types in action so you can avoid them.

DEBATABLE TOPICS

EXAMPLE

Sample Debatable Topic: Should students be allowed to record teachers during class?

Sample Response:

Some people might say that students should be allowed to record their teachers in class because it helps students learn better. They can replay lessons later to review tough material and double-check their notes for clarification. Plus, recordings can hold everyone accountable, which would get rid of any miscommunication that might happen between teachers and students.

On the other hand, some teachers believe that recording them is intrusive. They might feel judged instead of trusted and afraid of accidentally doing or saying the wrong thing. Plus, if recorded clips get shared online, they might be taken out of context which can damage reputations or cause drama nobody has time for.

A middle ground might be that students could be allowed to record lectures with permission or when they have a legitimate learning reason. Teachers could set clear rules about how recordings are used and shared, and maybe even require a personal contract so everyone feels respected and protected.

The goal should be to learn and teach in classrooms where education comes first and everyone feels safe.

DEBATABLE TOPICS

CONSIDER TWO OR MORE SIDES OF A CONTROVERSIAL SUBJECT.

1. Should we, as a society, punish people who use illegal drugs?

_____

_____

_____

_____

_____

_____

_____

_____

_____

_____

_____

_____

_____

_____

_____

_____

_____

_____

_____

_____

_____

_____

_____

DEBATABLE TOPICS

CONSIDER TWO OR MORE SIDES OF A CONTROVERSIAL SUBJECT.

2. Should the people of the United States continue to vote for a two-party political system?

_____

_____

_____

_____

_____

_____

_____

_____

_____

_____

_____

_____

_____

_____

_____

_____

_____

_____

_____

_____

_____

_____

_____

_____

_____

_____

_____

DEBATABLE TOPICS

CONSIDER TWO OR MORE SIDES OF A CONTROVERSIAL SUBJECT.

3. Should a federal government provide healthcare for all its citizens?

_____

_____

_____

_____

_____

_____

_____

_____

_____

_____

_____

_____

_____

_____

_____

_____

_____

_____

_____

_____

_____

_____

_____

DEBATABLE TOPICS

CONSIDER TWO OR MORE SIDES OF A CONTROVERSIAL SUBJECT.

4. Should the United States increase its commitment to renewable energy?

_____

_____

_____

_____

_____

_____

_____

_____

_____

_____

_____

_____

_____

_____

_____

_____

_____

_____

_____

_____

_____

_____

_____

_____

_____

_____

DEBATABLE TOPICS

CONSIDER TWO OR MORE SIDES OF A CONTROVERSIAL SUBJECT.

5. Should every teenager be required to take a semester of a class on social media literacy to better understand concepts such as bias in posts and social media etiquette?

_____

_____

_____

_____

_____

_____

_____

_____

_____

_____

_____

_____

_____

_____

_____

_____

_____

_____

_____

_____

_____

_____

_____

DEBATABLE TOPICS

CONSIDER TWO OR MORE SIDES OF A CONTROVERSIAL SUBJECT.

6. Should animal testing be allowed if it saves the lives of humans?

_____

_____

_____

_____

_____

_____

_____

_____

_____

_____

_____

_____

_____

_____

_____

_____

_____

_____

_____

_____

_____

_____

_____

_____

DEBATABLE TOPICS

CONSIDER TWO OR MORE SIDES OF A CONTROVERSIAL SUBJECT.

7. Should cigarettes be banned in the United States?

_____

_____

_____

_____

_____

_____

_____

_____

_____

_____

_____

_____

_____

_____

_____

_____

_____

_____

_____

_____

_____

_____

DEBATABLE TOPICS

CONSIDER TWO OR MORE SIDES OF A CONTROVERSIAL SUBJECT.

8. Should people who are worth a billion dollars be required to pay more taxes than those who make under $100,000?

_____

_____

_____

_____

_____

_____

_____

_____

_____

_____

_____

_____

_____

_____

_____

_____

_____

_____

_____

_____

_____

_____

_____

DEBATABLE TOPICS

CONSIDER TWO OR MORE SIDES OF A CONTROVERSIAL SUBJECT.

9. Should teenagers be allowed to get tattoos without parental consent?

_____

_____

_____

_____

_____

_____

_____

_____

_____

_____

_____

_____

_____

_____

_____

_____

_____

_____

_____

_____

_____

_____

DEBATABLE TOPICS

CONSIDER TWO OR MORE SIDES OF A CONTROVERSIAL SUBJECT.

10. Should teachers or schools ban or remove certain books from their libraries?

_____

_____

_____

_____

_____

_____

_____

_____

_____

_____

_____

_____

_____

_____

_____

_____

_____

_____

_____

_____

_____

_____

_____

DEBATABLE TOPICS

CONSIDER TWO OR MORE SIDES OF A CONTROVERSIAL SUBJECT.

11. Should there be a regulatory body for the usage of AI in society?

_____

_____

_____

_____

_____

_____

_____

_____

_____

_____

_____

_____

_____

_____

_____

_____

_____

_____

_____

_____

_____

_____

_____

DEBATABLE TOPICS

CONSIDER TWO OR MORE SIDES OF A CONTROVERSIAL SUBJECT.

12. Should all students be given art and music education while in high school?

DEBATABLE TOPICS

CONSIDER TWO OR MORE SIDES OF A CONTROVERSIAL SUBJECT.

13. Should military drafts be instated during wartime?

_____

_____

_____

_____

_____

_____

_____

_____

_____

_____

_____

_____

_____

_____

_____

_____

_____

_____

_____

_____

_____

_____

DEBATABLE TOPICS

CONSIDER TWO OR MORE SIDES OF A CONTROVERSIAL SUBJECT.

14. Should teenagers have unrestricted access to birth control?

DEBATABLE TOPICS

CONSIDER TWO OR MORE SIDES OF A CONTROVERSIAL SUBJECT.

15. Should parents be held legally responsible for their children's crimes?

_____

_____

_____

_____

_____

_____

_____

_____

_____

_____

_____

_____

_____

_____

_____

_____

_____

_____

_____

_____

_____

_____

DEBATABLE TOPICS

CONSIDER TWO OR MORE SIDES OF A CONTROVERSIAL SUBJECT.

16. Should schools be allowed to monitor students' social media accounts?

_____

_____

_____

_____

_____

_____

_____

_____

_____

_____

_____

_____

_____

_____

_____

_____

_____

_____

_____

_____

_____

_____

_____

DEBATABLE TOPICS

CONSIDER TWO OR MORE SIDES OF A CONTROVERSIAL SUBJECT.

17. Should the U.S. government provide monetary reparations for slavery?

_____

_____

_____

_____

_____

_____

_____

_____

_____

_____

_____

_____

_____

_____

_____

_____

_____

_____

_____

_____

_____

_____

_____

DEBATABLE TOPICS

CONSIDER TWO OR MORE SIDES OF A CONTROVERSIAL SUBJECT.

18. Should social media companies be responsible for misinformation posted on their platforms?

_____

_____

_____

_____

_____

_____

_____

_____

_____

_____

_____

_____

_____

_____

_____

_____

_____

_____

_____

_____

_____

_____

_____

_____

DEBATABLE TOPICS

CONSIDER TWO OR MORE SIDES OF A CONTROVERSIAL SUBJECT.

19. Should the U.S. lower the voting age to 16?

_____

_____

_____

_____

_____

_____

_____

_____

_____

_____

_____

_____

_____

_____

_____

_____

_____

_____

_____

_____

_____

_____

_____

DEBATABLE TOPICS

CONSIDER TWO OR MORE SIDES OF A CONTROVERSIAL SUBJECT.

20. Should felons have the right to vote after serving their sentences?

POETRY

RHYMING LINES

COMPLETE THE RHYMING POEM.

WHAT IS POETRY?

French poet Paul Valéry once said that if prose (ordinary writing without rhythm or structure) is walking, then poetry is dancing. Simply put, a poem is a type of literature that tells a story or shares an idea in a rhythmic, lyrical, aesthetic way. Rather than complete sentences and full paragraphs, poetry uses lines, stanzas, verses, meter, rhythm, word choice, and an entire suitcase of literary devices like metaphor, alliteration, and simile to grab a reader's heart and shake it around.

Most songs you listen to on repeat are rhyming poetry, and many of them have found that magical way to combine rhyme with meter and emotion to make you *feel something*, which is the whole point of poetry.

HOW DO YOU WRITE A RHYMING POEM?

The same way you fall in love—by listening to the thrumming of your heart, putting your brain in your pocket and zipping it closed, and finding a rhythm and rhyme pattern that moves you. Easy. (Ha!) It might not be simple, but if you're stuck at the end of one of these rhyming poems and aren't sure how to continue, do this: read it out loud to hear the rhythm, then make a list of rhyming words that fit the pattern to see if one of them stands out. Finally, pretend you're someone who *does* write poetry and give it your very best shot.

TIP: UNDERSTANDING RHYME SCHEMES

Many rhyming poems follow a particular *rhyme scheme*, the predictable pattern of rhymes at the ends of the lines. One way to show the pattern is with letters to the left of each line. For example:

A Romance is **great**
B Cherries are <u>sweet</u>
A You showed up **late**
B Now you're on the <u>street</u>

Here, the ends of the A lines rhyme with each other as do the ends of the B lines. Other stanzas could continue this pattern of ABAB, rhyming new 1st and 3rd lines with great/late and 2nd and 4th lines with sweet/street, or they could move on to new rhyming words in a CDCD, ACAC, or even other patterns. Some lines will have no rhyming pattern, which is indicated by an "X."

141

RHYMING LINES

COMPLETE THE RHYMING POEM.

Sample Rhyming Line:

A Hot off the press and broadcast the news
A Somebody call the hosts from The View
B A flash of that handsome face on the screen
B

Sample Response:

A Hot off the press and broadcast the news
A Somebody call the hosts from The View
B A flash of that handsome face on the screen
B They just didn't know he was mine, to me

C I thought he was endless, a circle of light
C A river of beauty, a star-filled night
D A pair of worn sneakers, a freckle-faced smile
D Who knew that I was wrong by a mile

E He said goodbye one rain-soaked day
E With a tease and a hug and a promise to stay
F I would have told him my feelings, I swear it, I swear
F If I'd only known he wouldn't be there

G Lay me down, rest my head, leave that seed unsown
G The price of my silence is my debt to atone
H He was my dawn, my noontime, my setting sun
H I just didn't know then that he was the one

RHYMING LINES

COMPLETE THE RHYMING POEM.

1.
A Should the pain be left unspoken?
B My mind goes round and round
A I'm battered, bruised and broken
B

_____

_____

_____

_____

_____

_____

_____

_____

_____

_____

_____

_____

_____

_____

_____

_____

_____

_____

_____

_____

_____

_____

RHYMING LINES

COMPLETE THE RHYMING POEM.

2.

A I've tried to tell you honestly the things that plague my mind
A But still I struggle for the words I cannot seem to find.
B I've tried at least a dozen times to tell you all my fears,
B

_____

_____

_____

_____

_____

_____

_____

_____

_____

_____

_____

_____

_____

_____

_____

_____

_____

_____

_____

_____

_____

_____

RHYMING LINES

COMPLETE THE RHYMING POEM.

3.
A You think that I don't see right through you
B When you cry and beg and plead
A You think your words are slick and blue
B

_____

_____

_____

_____

_____

_____

_____

_____

_____

_____

_____

_____

_____

_____

_____

_____

_____

_____

_____

_____

_____

_____

RHYMING LINES

COMPLETE THE RHYMING POEM.

4.
A I did not let it spin and spin
B the whirlwind of my clustered mind
C I sat right down and plucked a rose
B

_____

_____

_____

_____

_____

_____

_____

_____

_____

_____

_____

_____

_____

_____

_____

_____

_____

_____

_____

_____

RHYMING LINES

COMPLETE THE RHYMING POEM.

5.
A "I have to paint the house," he said.
B "In blue and green and goldenrod."
C "I have to paint the house, my love"
B

_____

_____

_____

_____

_____

_____

_____

_____

_____

_____

_____

_____

_____

_____

_____

_____

_____

_____

_____

_____

_____

_____

_____

RHYMING LINES

COMPLETE THE RHYMING POEM.

6.

A Lying asleep, curled up, unseen
B I drift away to worlds unknown
B Seeds of thought that have been sown
A

_____

_____

_____

_____

_____

_____

_____

_____

_____

_____

_____

_____

_____

_____

_____

_____

_____

_____

_____

_____

_____

_____

RHYMING LINES

COMPLETE THE RHYMING POEM.

7.
A Imagine that. Stooped so low, I couldn't see ya
B Imagine spitting all that game and no one cares
A Imagine thinking that you're any part of me, yeah
B

_____

_____

_____

_____

_____

_____

_____

_____

_____

_____

_____

_____

_____

_____

_____

_____

_____

_____

_____

_____

_____

_____

_____

_____

RHYMING LINES

COMPLETE THE RHYMING POEM.

8.

A In the middle of the deepest night
B When ships sink fast and oceans roar
A Stars still shine with fervent light
B

_____

_____

_____

_____

_____

_____

_____

_____

_____

_____

_____

_____

_____

_____

_____

_____

_____

_____

_____

_____

RHYMING LINES

COMPLETE THE RHYMING POEM

9.
A We have become a moment of joy
B Her hand holds mine with every sip
C And just before the flash goes off
B

_____

_____

_____

_____

_____

_____

_____

_____

_____

_____

_____

_____

_____

_____

_____

_____

_____

_____

_____

_____

_____

_____

_____

RHYMING LINES

COMPLETE THE RHYMING POEM.

10.
A They ask "How did you meet?"
B And I tell 'em how it was
A We were walking down the street
A

_____

_____

_____

_____

_____

_____

_____

_____

_____

_____

_____

_____

_____

_____

_____

_____

_____

_____

_____

RHYMING LINES

COMPLETE THE RHYMING POEM.

11.
A Ravaged by the winter wind
A the bird's a stone, as if pinned
B to the line that shakes like bones
B

_____

_____

_____

_____

_____

_____

_____

_____

_____

_____

_____

_____

_____

_____

_____

_____

_____

_____

_____

_____

RHYMING LINES

COMPLETE THE RHYMING POEM.

12.

A In vengeful fields of flowering red
B A single shot cracks through the breeze
B It begs please mercy mercy please
A

_____

_____

_____

_____

_____

_____

_____

_____

_____

_____

_____

_____

_____

_____

_____

_____

_____

_____

_____

_____

RHYMING LINES

COMPLETE THE RHYMING POEM.

13.
A When the sun gives up the ghost
B and all have fled the confines of
C their graves to fly o'er mountaintops
B

_____

_____

_____

_____

_____

_____

_____

_____

_____

_____

_____

_____

_____

_____

_____

_____

_____

_____

_____

_____

_____

RHYMING LINES

COMPLETE THE RHYMING POEM.

14

A She wrote a letter to her mom and signed it with an X and O
A then sealed it in an envelope and placed it down beside her hopes
B She drove away to Kalamazoo, the place where it had all began
B

_____

_____

_____

_____

_____

_____

_____

_____

_____

_____

_____

_____

_____

_____

_____

_____

_____

_____

_____

_____

RHYMING LINES

COMPLETE THE RHYMING POEM.

15.

A I pray your hair falls out the second that you comb it

B I pray you lose your wallet and somebody steals your cash

A I pray you buy a house, but you don't own it

B

_____

_____

_____

_____

_____

_____

_____

_____

_____

_____

_____

_____

_____

_____

_____

_____

_____

_____

_____

_____

_____

_____

_____

_____

RHYMING LINES

COMPLETE THE RHYMING POEM.

16.
A Cars crash, it's just how things go
B *But not hers,* my brain says when I'm tired
A You'd begged her that day to drive real slow
B

_____

_____

_____

_____

_____

_____

_____

_____

_____

_____

_____

_____

_____

_____

_____

_____

_____

_____

_____

_____

_____

RHYMING LINES

COMPLETE THE RHYMING POEM.

17.
X Don't let the bitterness destroy you
A Their words don't mean a thing
X That monster wants your sanity
A

_____

_____

_____

_____

_____

_____

_____

_____

_____

_____

_____

_____

_____

_____

_____

_____

_____

_____

_____

_____

_____

_____

RHYMING LINES
COMPLETE THE RHYMING POEM.

18.
A Kiss me now underneath the streetlight
A Make it slow, I want to get it just right
A Talk is cheap, but I feel the truth this night
B

_____

_____

_____

_____

_____

_____

_____

_____

_____

_____

_____

_____

_____

_____

_____

_____

_____

_____

_____

_____

RHYMING LINES

COMPLETE THE RHYMING POEM.

19.
A If you save a bird that flies in your window
B Your life has been well lived
C It's not always the big things that add up to greatness
B

_____

_____

_____

_____

_____

_____

_____

_____

_____

_____

_____

_____

_____

_____

_____

_____

_____

_____

_____

_____

_____

_____

RHYMING LINES

COMPLETE THE RHYMING POEM.

20.
A Follow the path, but go the good way
B Don't veer to the left or the right
A Troubles will come when you're looking away
B

_____

_____

_____

_____

_____

_____

_____

_____

_____

_____

_____

_____

_____

_____

_____

_____

_____

_____

_____

_____

FREE VERSE LYRICS

COMPLETE THE FREE VERSE POEM.

WHAT IS FREE VERSE?

Free verse poetry is has no regular meter or rhyme and tends to follow the natural rhythm of speaking. It gives poets the freedom to explore other parts of poetic writing like alliteration, cadence, internal rhyme, repetition, symbolism, line spacing, and other literary devices to rip the reader's heart out and throw it against the wall.

Free verse poetry is often profound in the emotion it can evoke. Poets from Poet Laureate Amanda Gorman to physician William Carlos Williams have perfected the art of shaping a small collection of words into electricity.

HOW DO YOU COMPLETE SOMEONE ELSE'S FREE VERSE POEM?

Free verse is about observation—observing your emotion about something that happened and perhaps a few of the physical details surrounding that event. To finish the poems that have been started for you, try these steps:

- **Write an emotion you feel as you read the lines.** If you don't feel anything, choose an emotion you *want* to feel.
- **Think of three physical objects that relate to the lines that are already there.** Jot them in the margins of the page. They could be symbolic of the feeling of the poem, could relate to a story you'd like to tell, or could have personal meaning to you.
- **Choose one of those objects to put into the poem.** Write a sentence with it in there, an emotion that relates, and then take out any word that doesn't zing.

TIP: USING CONNOTATION

Connotation, or using a word to suggest a different association than its literal meaning, is vital in free verse poetry.

For example, the word "fire" means burning. That's its *denotative,* or literal meaning. But it's *connotative,* or suggested meaning, can be a variety of things. Fire can suggest passion or anger or even enjoyment.
After you finish the poem, go back and make sure each word is used to its fullest by thinking through its connotation.
Sure, blue is blue, but if your poem is about happiness, should you swap blue out for gold? Or sunshine yellow?

FREE VERSE LYRICS
COMPLETE THE FREE VERSE POEM.

Sample Free Verse Lyric:

I choke as shame goes down my throat
Flushed by the dirty acid waves
of aluminum fizz

You'll need...

Sample Response:
I choke as shame goes down my throat
flushed by the dirty acid waves
of aluminum fizz

You'll need some help for this kind of pain, the moss-eyed counselor tells me

but my ears hear penance because that's how you don't burn
chastise, flog, flagellate, punish before they punish you

I pull out the cat o' nines,
give myself six stripes for forgetting she was my sister
a dozen more for each time I let them hurt her
at least one million for not screaming
         louder when cops asked me if she was okay

burn me at the stake I want to be FRIED by my own shame, by my own silence
my heart sinks low in my body, a cephalopod, slimy and burrowing deep inside its mud brown shell

no help for me
no absolution of my sin
no cross that can save me from myself
from the knowledge that it was all my fault

No, she says
Not your fault

That's on your parents.

FREE VERSE LYRICS

COMPLETE THE FREE VERSE POEM.

1.

Fire burns me up
Exploding through my veins
Sparks of lightning electrocuting action
I jump...

_____

_____

_____

_____

_____

_____

_____

_____

_____

_____

_____

_____

_____

_____

_____

_____

_____

_____

_____

_____

_____

FREE VERSE LYRICS

COMPLETE THE FREE VERSE POEM.

2.

Swimming underwater
skinny dipping in moonlight
throaty rumbles pull me up to midnight

Breaking the surface... _____
_____
_____
_____
_____
_____
_____
_____
_____
_____
_____
_____
_____
_____
_____
_____
_____
_____
_____
_____

FREE VERSE LYRICS

COMPLETE THE FREE VERSE POEM.

3.
Beacons burn on the light posts
a path back to the safety of my bed
in a house where they want me. Where
the dog and the photos of my childhood
always...

_____

_____

_____

_____

_____

_____

_____

_____

_____

_____

_____

_____

_____

_____

_____

_____

_____

_____

_____

_____

FREE VERSE LYRICS

COMPLETE THE FREE VERSE POEM.

4
We yank the bass up high
booms rattling in our chest
the ice cubes of our dad's disappointment
melting into the...

_____

_____

_____

_____

_____

_____

_____

_____

_____

_____

_____

_____

_____

_____

_____

_____

_____

_____

_____

_____

_____

_____

_____

FREE VERSE LYRICS

COMPLETE THE FREE VERSE POEM.

5.

I am
a window cracked to let in
the fresh salt sea at dawn
I am...

_____

_____

_____

_____

_____

_____

_____

_____

_____

_____

_____

_____

_____

_____

_____

_____

_____

_____

_____

_____

_____

FREE VERSE LYRICS

COMPLETE THE FREE VERSE POEM.

6.

I broke away in my striped convict costume
one hand in the Pop Tarts, the other flipping everyone I left behind the bird

My grandma's rosary swings from the rearview mirror.
She never saw my...

_____

_____

_____

_____

_____

_____

_____

_____

_____

_____

_____

_____

_____

_____

_____

_____

_____

_____

_____

_____

_____

FREE VERSE LYRICS

COMPLETE THE FREE VERSE POEM.

7.
You gave me your music mind
hands that can turn ordinary into art
eyes that see the birds and the stars and are enraptured by both
ears that...

_____

_____

_____

_____

_____

_____

_____

_____

_____

_____

_____

_____

_____

_____

_____

_____

_____

_____

_____

_____

_____

FREE VERSE LYRICS

COMPLETE THE FREE VERSE POEM.

8.
She
Holds kindness in her hands
like a bird
and releases it to the world,
so they can see it
green and gold in the
azure sky.

She...

_____

_____

_____

_____

_____

_____

_____

_____

_____

_____

_____

_____

_____

_____

_____

_____

_____

_____

FREE VERSE LYRICS

COMPLETE THE FREE VERSE POEM.

9.
You're tangy.
But you only taste that way to me because I know you
I've felt the twist at the tip of my tongue as you,
citrus sweet-tart,
wink with piquant eyes

To everyone else..

_____

_____

_____

_____

_____

_____

_____

_____

_____

_____

_____

_____

_____

_____

_____

_____

_____

_____

_____

_____

_____

FREE VERSE LYRICS

COMPLETE THE FREE VERSE POEM.

10.
He's gone and I'm here, hating sunshine
I snik closed the shades, shutting it out.
By the door,...

_____

_____

_____

_____

_____

_____

_____

_____

_____

_____

_____

_____

_____

_____

_____

_____

_____

_____

_____

_____

_____

FREE VERSE LYRICS

COMPLETE THE FREE VERSE POEM.

11.

People look to the sun
for light
Stare at the bright showers of sparks
beating heavy on their backs
But not me...

_____

_____

_____

_____

_____

_____

_____

_____

_____

_____

_____

_____

_____

_____

_____

_____

_____

_____

_____

_____

FREE VERSE LYRICS

COMPLETE THE FREE VERSE POEM.

12.

I can't imagine this road without you
Don't even want to try
Even when the dust has gotten
so bad
we...

_____

_____

_____

_____

_____

_____

_____

_____

_____

_____

_____

_____

_____

_____

_____

_____

_____

_____

_____

_____

FREE VERSE LYRICS

COMPLETE THE FREE VERSE POEM.

13.
I wish I could
paper his patience
all over your walls
smooth the yellow rosebuds
over the gray cracks and...

_____

_____

_____

_____

_____

_____

_____

_____

_____

_____

_____

_____

_____

_____

_____

_____

_____

_____

_____

_____

_____

_____

FREE VERSE LYRICS

COMPLETE THE FREE VERSE POEM.

14.
Lies circle like gnats
around my blue lamp
frantic
in the electricity of my knowledge
You...

_____

_____

_____

_____

_____

_____

_____

_____

_____

_____

_____

_____

_____

_____

_____

_____

_____

_____

_____

_____

FREE VERSE LYRICS

COMPLETE THE FREE VERSE POEM.

15.
Cover me, my mother, with stones
For in this sickly hour
My bones are exposed to dusk
and you...

FREE VERSE LYRICS

COMPLETE THE FREE VERSE POEM.

16.
Real silence is what happens
when the power fizzles out
Then, you hear the earth
as it...

_____

_____

_____

_____

_____

_____

_____

_____

_____

_____

_____

_____

_____

_____

_____

_____

_____

_____

FREE VERSE LYRICS

COMPLETE THE FREE VERSE POEM.

17.
I swallowed my voice
so you could speak
that one December morning
It tasted so...

_____

_____

_____

_____

_____

_____

_____

_____

_____

_____

_____

_____

_____

_____

_____

_____

_____

_____

_____

_____

_____

_____

FREE VERSE LYRICS

COMPLETE THE FREE VERSE POEM.

18.
Mallorca called me to its sheltered coves
that hide from the breaking sea
the diamond waves glittered until
they...

_____

_____

_____

_____

_____

_____

_____

_____

_____

_____

_____

_____

_____

_____

_____

_____

_____

_____

_____

_____

FREE VERSE LYRICS

COMPLETE THE FREE VERSE POEM.

19.
Splash on the blacktop
wheels spinning close,
 spitting up rocks - pepper spraying me

I'm hauled like...

_____
_____
_____
_____
_____
_____
_____
_____
_____
_____
_____
_____
_____
_____
_____
_____
_____
_____
_____
_____
_____

FREE VERSE LYRICS

COMPLETE THE FREE VERSE POEM.

20.

His leather coat buttons chill my cheeks,
cologne blooms up my nose
His diamond earring shines like a meteor
that's crashing through...

_____

_____

_____

_____

_____

_____

_____

_____

_____

_____

_____

_____

_____

_____

_____

_____

_____

_____

_____

_____

_____

RHYTHMIC TRIOS

WRITE A RHYTHMIC POEM INCLUDING THE THREE GIVEN WORDS.

Regular meter isn't required for poetry with or without three words to include in your poem, but it can be helpful to know about it if your poem sounds "off" and you can't figure out why. Meter is made up of *feet*, which have nothing to do with what you shove into your shoes. In a line of rhythmic poetry, a single *foot* has **a certain number of syllables** and a particular **pattern of emphasis on those syllables**. Repeat those a bunch and you have the meter.

Let's get to know a few of these kinds of feet. The names aren't important, but if your ears can grasp the patterns of each, you'll have an easier time writing a rhythmic poem.

WHAT ARE SOME COMMON METRIC FEET?

- **anapest:** Syllable emphasis is *bum-bum-BUM* like, "contradict." Here's a poetic line using anapestic meter: "When I wake in the morning, it's like I'm alone." If you say it aloud, you can hear the meter. When I WAKE in the MORNing, it's LIKE I'm aLONE.

- **dactyl:** Syllable emphasis is *BUM-bum-bum* like "basketball." Say it aloud: "Rhythm of poetry, sing us a song." RHYthm of POetry, SING us a SONG.

- **iamb:** Syllable emphasis is *bum-BUM* like "invest." Say it aloud: "I want to listen to the wind." i WANT to LISten TO the WIND.

- **trochee:** Syllable emphasis is *BUM-bum* like "snowball." Say it aloud: "Sit down. Let me tell it true." SIT down. LET me TELL it TRUE.

TIP: FIGURING OUT METER

If you use one foot per line you're using *monometer*. Two is *dimeter*, three is *trimeter*, four is *tetrameter*, five is *pentameter*, six is *hexameter*, seven is *heptameter*, eight is *octometer*, and so on.

If you add the type of foot you used with the number of times you used it, you can identify the rhythm precisely. For instance, five iambs per line is *iambic pentameter*. Two anapests per line is *anapestic dimeter*.
"When I WAKE in the MORNing, it's LIKE I'm aLONE" is an example of anapestic tetrameter.
"SIT down. LET me TELL it TRUE" is an example of trochaic tetrameter (minus the last unstressed syllable).

RHYTHMIC TRIOS

WRITE A RHYTHMIC POEM INCLUDING THE THREE GIVEN WORDS.

Sample Rhythmic Trio:

iambic tetrameter

Flashlight
Click
Hot

Sample Response:

Unrhymed:
The **flashlight** trembles in my hand.
I **click** once more to find the path.
The glow is **hot**; the trees are still.
A single moth dissolves in light.

The ground is soft beneath my feet.
A sound unfolds beyond the beam.
I **click** again—the dark arrives.
The cold collects beneath my skin.

The flashlight hums, a dying star.
The forest sways but does not speak.
The air stays quiet, silence deep.
I walk until the light is gone.

Rhymed:
The **flashlight** cold against my hand,
I know I'll need it for this land.
I **click** it on, the woods awake,
Their whispers coiled up like a snake.

The air is **hot**, a monstrous thing,
It clings to skin, a serpent's sting.
The night is thick, the stars withdrawn,
The pulse of heat keeps pressing on.

The beam clicks off. Oh no! I say.
The angry dark is here to stay.
I wait for creatures big and small
But all I feel is nature's call

Of trembling shadows folding in
The hot earth humming soft as wind.

TIP: IF YOU CAN'T NAIL THE RHYTHMIC PATTERN:

Skip it.
Try to write your poem using the rhythm provided.

BUT!

If you can't make it work or it's stressing you out,
then simply come up with your own
rhythmic pattern and write a poem
using the given trio with that. ;-)

Remember: it can be rhymed or unrhymed and you
can end a line in the middle of
one of the rhythmic feet. No problem at all.

RHYTHMIC TRIOS

WRITE A RHYTHMIC POEM INCLUDING THE THREE GIVEN WORDS.

1.

iambic tetrameter (bum-BUM bum-BUM bum-BUM bum-BUM)

Awake

Juice

Crisp

_____

_____

_____

_____

_____

_____

_____

_____

_____

_____

_____

_____

_____

_____

_____

_____

_____

_____

_____

_____

_____

_____

_____

RHYTHMIC TRIOS

WRITE A RHYTHMIC POEM INCLUDING THE THREE GIVEN WORDS.

2.

anapestic tetrameter (bum-bum-BUM bum-bum-BUM bum-bum-BUM bum-bum-BUM)
Boom
Contradict
Press

_____

_____

_____

_____

_____

_____

_____

_____

_____

_____

_____

_____

_____

_____

_____

_____

_____

_____

_____

_____

_____

RHYTHMIC TRIOS

WRITE A RHYTHMIC POEM INCLUDING THE THREE GIVEN WORDS.

3.
iambic pentameter (bum-BUM bum-BUM bum-BUM bum-BUM bum-BUM)

Invest
Love
Drink

_____

_____

_____

_____

_____

_____

_____

_____

_____

_____

_____

_____

_____

_____

_____

_____

_____

_____

_____

_____

_____

_____

RHYTHMIC TRIOS

WRITE A RHYTHMIC POEM INCLUDING THE THREE GIVEN WORDS.

4
dactylic dimeter (BUM-bum-bum BUM-bum-bum)
Patty cake
String
Cash

_____

_____

_____

_____

_____

_____

_____

_____

_____

_____

_____

_____

_____

_____

_____

_____

_____

_____

_____

_____

_____

RHYTHMIC TRIOS

WRITE A RHYTHMIC POEM INCLUDING THE THREE GIVEN WORDS.

5.
anapestic dimeter (bum-bum-BUM bum-bum-BUM)
Blue
Snake
Mountain

RHYTHMIC TRIOS

WRITE A RHYTHMIC POEM INCLUDING THE THREE GIVEN WORDS.

6.

dactylic tetrameter (BUM-bum-bum BUM-bum-bum BUM-bum-bum BUM-bum-bum)

Beautiful

Heart

Crush

_____

_____

_____

_____

_____

_____

_____

_____

_____

_____

_____

_____

_____

_____

_____

_____

_____

_____

_____

_____

_____

RHYTHMIC TRIOS

WRITE A RHYTHMIC POEM INCLUDING THE THREE GIVEN WORDS.

7.
iambic dimeter (bum-BUM bum-BUM)
Begin
Wise
Branch

_____

_____

_____

_____

_____

_____

_____

_____

_____

_____

_____

_____

_____

_____

_____

_____

_____

_____

_____

_____

_____

_____

_____

_____

RHYTHMIC TRIOS

WRITE A RHYTHMIC POEM INCLUDING THE THREE GIVEN WORDS.

8.

trochaic tetrameter (BUM-bum BUM-bum BUM-bum BUM-bum)

Shadow

Blood

Black

_____

_____

_____

_____

_____

_____

_____

_____

_____

_____

_____

_____

_____

_____

_____

_____

_____

_____

_____

_____

_____

RHYTHMIC TRIOS

WRITE A RHYTHMIC POEM INCLUDING THE THREE GIVEN WORDS.

9.
anapestic trimeter (bum-bum-BUM bum-bum-BUM bum-bum-BUM)
Understand
Clank
Night

_____

_____

_____

_____

_____

_____

_____

_____

_____

_____

_____

_____

_____

_____

_____

_____

_____

_____

_____

_____

_____

_____

RHYTHMIC TRIOS

WRITE A RHYTHMIC POEM INCLUDING THE THREE GIVEN WORDS.

10.
iambic pentameter (bum-BUM bum-BUM bum-BUM bum-BUM bum-BUM)
Restore
Blink
Path

_____

_____

_____

_____

_____

_____

_____

_____

_____

_____

_____

_____

_____

_____

_____

_____

_____

_____

_____

_____

_____

RHYTHMIC TRIOS

WRITE A RHYTHMIC POEM INCLUDING THE THREE GIVEN WORDS.

11.
trochaic trimeter (BUM-bum BUM-bum BUM-bum)
Mangle
Crowd
Leg

_____

_____

_____

_____

_____

_____

_____

_____

_____

_____

_____

_____

_____

_____

_____

_____

_____

_____

_____

_____

_____

_____

RHYTHMIC TRIOS

WRITE A RHYTHMIC POEM INCLUDING THE THREE GIVEN WORDS.

12.
iambic trimeter (bum-BUM bum-BUM bum-BUM)
Reclaim
Dust
Sea

_____

_____

_____

_____

_____

_____

_____

_____

_____

_____

_____

_____

_____

_____

_____

_____

_____

_____

_____

_____

RHYTHMIC TRIOS

WRITE A RHYTHMIC POEM INCLUDING THE THREE GIVEN WORDS.

13.
trochaic trimeter (BUM-bum BUM-bum BUM-bum)
Winter
Flame
Climb

_____

_____

_____

_____

_____

_____

_____

_____

_____

_____

_____

_____

_____

_____

_____

_____

_____

_____

_____

_____

_____

_____

RHYTHMIC TRIOS

WRITE A RHYTHMIC POEM INCLUDING THE THREE GIVEN WORDS.

14.

anapestic pentameter (bum-bum-BUM bum-bum-BUM bum-bum-BUM bum-bum-BUM bum-bum-BUM)

Understand

Clash

Light

RHYTHMIC TRIOS

WRITE A RHYTHMIC POEM INCLUDING THE THREE GIVEN WORDS.

15.
trochaic pentameter (BUM-bum BUM-bum BUM-bum BUM-bum BUM-bum)
Roses
Mine
Gold

RHYTHMIC TRIOS

WRITE A RHYTHMIC POEM INCLUDING THE THREE GIVEN WORDS.

16.
dactylic trimeter (BUM-bum-bum BUM-bum-bum BUM-bum-bum)
Butterfly
Grass
Breathe

_____

_____

_____

_____

_____

_____

_____

_____

_____

_____

_____

_____

_____

_____

_____

_____

_____

_____

_____

_____

_____

_____

RHYTHMIC TRIOS

WRITE A RHYTHMIC POEM INCLUDING THE THREE GIVEN WORDS.

17.
iambic tetrameter (bum-BUM bum-BUM bum-BUM bum-BUM)
Betray
Bone
Leash

_____

_____

_____

_____

_____

_____

_____

_____

_____

_____

_____

_____

_____

_____

_____

_____

_____

_____

_____

_____

_____

_____

RHYTHMIC TRIOS

WRITE A RHYTHMIC POEM INCLUDING THE THREE GIVEN WORDS.

18.

trochaic tetrameter (BUM-bum BUM-bum BUM-bum BUM-bum)

Morning

Salt

Rain

_____

_____

_____

_____

_____

_____

_____

_____

_____

_____

_____

_____

_____

_____

_____

_____

_____

_____

_____

_____

RHYTHMIC TRIOS

WRITE A RHYTHMIC POEM INCLUDING THE THREE GIVEN WORDS.

19.
dactylic tetrameter (BUM-bum-bum BUM-bum-bum BUM-bum-bum BUM-bum-bum)
Terrible
Scream
Bird

_____

_____

_____

_____

_____

_____

_____

_____

_____

_____

_____

_____

_____

_____

_____

_____

_____

_____

_____

_____

_____

_____

RHYTHMIC TRIOS

WRITE A RHYTHMIC POEM INCLUDING THE THREE GIVEN WORDS.

20.
trochaic trimeter (BUM-bum BUM-bum BUM-bum)
Whisper
Moon
Seed

_____

_____

_____

_____

_____

_____

_____

_____

_____

_____

_____

_____

_____

_____

_____

_____

_____

_____

_____

_____

NOTES

NOTES

NOTES

NOTES

www.ingramcontent.com/pod-product-compliance
Lightning Source LLC
Chambersburg PA
CBHW080901120626
46555CB00008B/2902